When the
BLUES
Won't Go Away

When the
BLUES
Won't Go Away

New Approaches to Dysthymic Disorder
and Other Forms of Chronic Low-Grade Depression

ROBERT M. A. HIRSCHFELD, M.D.,
Professor and Chairman,
Department of Psychiatry and Behavioral Sciences,
The University of Texas Medical Branch at Galveston
with SUSAN MELTSNER

Produced by The Philip Lief Group, Inc.

Macmillan Publishing Company   New York

Maxwell Macmillan Canada   Toronto

Maxwell Macmillan International
New York   Oxford   Singapore   Sydney

Macmillan Publishing Company
866 Third Avenue
New York, NY 10022

Maxwell Macmillan Canada, Inc.
1200 Eglinton Avenue East, Suite 200
Don Mills, Ontario M3C 3N1

Macmillan Publishing Company is part of
the Maxwell Communication Group of Companies.

Produced by The Philip Lief Group, Inc.

This book is not intended as a substitute for the medical advice of physicians. The reader should consult a physician in matters relating to his or her health, particularly with respect to the symptoms described in this book.

The opinions expressed in this publication are the views of the authors and do not necessarily reflect the official position of the National Institute of Mental Health or any other part of the U.S. Department of Health and Human Services.

LIBRARY OF CONGRESS CATALOGING-IN-PUBLICATION DATA
Hirschfeld, Robert M. A.
    When the blues won't go away:new approaches to
dysthymic disorder and other forms of chronic low-grade
depression / Robert M. A. Hirschfeld.
        p.   cm.
    Includes bibliographical references and index.
    ISBN 0-02-551825-9
    1. Depression, Mental.   I. Title.
RC537.H564   1990
616.85'27—dc20   90-43269

This book is dedicated to all those who suffer from the blues,
especially those whose suffering has continued
for years without improvement.
It is hoped that
this book will help them
get better.

The people described in this book are not real.
Their background and experiences
are drawn from patients
I have treated.

Contents

Preface

This book is about a special kind of clinical depression—one that is long lasting and relatively mild. Mental health professionals refer to it as dysthymic disorder, or dysthymia (DD, for short).

A cluster of specific symptoms and their effects on your life distinguish DD from other forms of depression as well as from brief, everyday, run-of-the-mill bouts of the blues. Those symptoms—from how long your blue mood has lasted to the effect it has on your appetite and sleep patterns—are indicators that help mental health professionals diagnose the disorder and choose the appropriate treatment for it. Millions of Americans qualify for the diagnosis of DD. But even if you don't, you can still benefit from the information and advice in this book. It also addresses the concerns of the even larger group of people who are having trouble bouncing back after a loss or life crisis and who are in danger of developing dysthymic disorder. And if you are simply blue, out of sorts, or in a bad mood more frequently than you care to be, without knowing why or what you can do to remedy the situation, this book can help you figure out what is getting you down. It will show you what you can do to improve your outlook. It offers you a road map for recovery from a case of the blues that won't go away.

If someone close to you has been down in the dumps day after day for months or even years, this book can clear up a few mysteries and provide you with some practical suggestions for helping that person conquer a chronic case of the blues.

If the blues have lingered long enough or occurred often enough, you may have forgotten that they are an emotional state and not an irrefutable and unalterable fact of life. You may have come to believe that blue is just the way you are and will always be. That is untrue. Dysthymic disorder, and any long-lasting blue mood for that matter, can be overcome in a relatively short period of time. Self-help strategies and therapies tailor-made for such problems, antidepressant medications, and a combination of these approaches have all proven effective. People with DD do get better. In fact, whether they sought professional assistance or made a conscious effort to help themselves, all of the people you will read about in this book recovered once they recognized and understood what was wrong and what could be done about it.

Whether you have a case of the blues that won't go away or are involved with someone who does, the first step toward overcoming dysthymia (or contending with someone who has it) is understanding that

- DD is an illness and that blue moods as well as all the thoughts, feelings, and behaviors that accompany them are symptoms of that illness;
- some people are more susceptible to the blues than others, and there are reasons for this;

- blue moods are self-perpetuating, and the way you think, feel, act, and interact with other people while down in the dumps tends to keep you there;
- DD is treatable, and people recover from it (and you will learn how);
- there are a number of effective measures for beating the blues that you can begin to put to work immediately.

Drawing upon my own observations as a clinical researcher and the data collected by other researchers, I have compiled a comprehensive picture of dysthymia that is as up to date as possible. You will learn enough about DD and what can be done to overcome it to get you started on the road to recovery. The suggestions found throughout the book and the self-help program should be especially useful.

It may also help to know that you are not alone. Many DD sufferers and their close associates were interviewed and served as guinea pigs for various self-help strategies. Their actual experiences, details of their recovery, and many of their own words are recorded and will be, I hope, a source of inspiration and encouragement for you. For the sake of confidentiality, I have changed all names, occupations, and other identifying information. And for the sake of clarity and readability, in some instances I have combined several individuals' stories to create composite case examples.

Just reading this book will not cure you, but it can propel you in the right direction, show you how to help yourself if that is what you choose to do, and provide you with the impetus to try therapy or antidepressant medications (or both) if that is what you decide to do. But you are the most important ingredient in the formula for beating the blues. Your willingness to put the words you find on these pages into action is what can make the blues go away.

If you have been in a blue mood for a long time (or expended much energy trying to deal with someone who has DD), that willingness may be difficult to find at first. That's okay. This book will take you through a step-by-step process for overcoming DD, but you do not have to complete all of the steps in the time it takes to read the book.

To gain the maximum benefits from the material that follows, I suggest that you take the time to complete at least some of the exercises provided. Since many of them require some writing, you may want to obtain a notebook to keep nearby while you are reading.

Finally, because the first few chapters describe the rut you have gotten into and what you may have done to stay in that rut, you may find yourself feeling more depressed rather than less so. This is a natural and temporary reaction to confronting the realities of life under the influence of a chronic case of the blues. It is not a reason to give up or to castigate yourself over the way you thought, felt, or behaved in the past. Be kind to yourself and remember that understanding and facing the facts about DD, despite the discomfort it may cause you now, is the key to beating the blues and feeling better in the future.

1

Symptoms of Dysthymic Disorder

D D is a long-standing disturbance in the way you think, feel, act, relate to other people, and function in general. If you have been in a blue mood most of the time for two or more years and your mood has lifted for no more than two months at a time, there is a good chance you have DD. If you are like most DD sufferers, you will be unable to pinpoint what is making or keeping you blue.

Many features of DD resemble those of major depressions, but its symptoms are less severe and usually longer lasting. You continue to function at home and at work, although not enthusiastically or at the level you once did. Unfinished chores, neglected relationships, and projects that are postponed indefinitely are all evidence of the blues' impact on you. Unlike people in the throes of a major depressive episode, however, you do manage to get out of bed, attend to personal hygiene, go to work, and take care of daily chores.

In addition, DD sufferers may eat too much or too little, sleep too much or not enough, be low on energy, have poor self-esteem, find it difficult to concentrate or make decisions, and feel desperate or hopeless. Some also experience increased anxiety and alcohol or drug use.

According to a recent study conducted by the National Institute of Mental Health, 3 to 5 percent of all American adults suffer from this disorder. An even greater number are candidates for it. They are having trouble bouncing back from personal losses or disappointments and have not begun to feel like their old selves again even though six months or more have passed since the crisis occurred. These two groups add up to millions of men and women whose blues won't go away.

Although anyone can get DD, twice as many women as men have it. Unmarried persons of both genders and young people with low incomes are highly susceptible to it, as are men and women with a history of depression or alcoholism in their families. DD is a growing problem among children and adolescents, and if your marriage is in trouble, you are twenty-five times more likely to have a chronic case of the blues than someone in a more stable relationship.

CONNIE'S STORY

Feeling as if lead weights were attached to her limbs, Connie mustered just enough energy to silence her incessantly ringing alarm clock and then plopped back onto her pillows like a limp rag doll. Even after ten hours of sleep, she was still exhausted. Her back ached. Her head throbbed. Her entire body felt bruised and bloated. Connie wished she could spend the entire day in bed, where it was safe and warm and quiet, but she knew she would not. She had too many things to do.

"My life is just one thankless task after another," Connie said, with the ever-present weariness in her voice and the slowness of her motions supporting the claim she made the first time I interviewed her. "I'm only thirty-four," she groaned, "but I feel more like sixty."

Physically, Connie did not look much different from the energetic, fun-loving, and optimistic twenty-three-year-old she had been on her wedding day. Yes, she had gained a few extra pounds over the years, and yes, there were a few wrinkles on her face, a few strands of premature gray in her sleek dark hair. But she was still a striking woman whose big brown eyes sparkled when she smiled. Regrettably, that smile was rarely seen anymore on her heart-shaped face, and Connie herself seldom saw the bright side of anything.

When Connie's husband, Dan, a thirty-five-year-old regional sales manager for a large insurance company, bounced out of bed and began humming a cheerful tune, Connie wanted to throw something at him and scream, "What the heck is there to hum about?" Instead, with a wave of guilt hitting her, she pulled the covers up over her head. "I have no right to be annoyed with Dan," she reminded herself. "I don't deserve someone so kind, patient, and understanding. It's a miracle he puts up with me at all." The sound of Dan waking their six- and seven-year-old sons only added to Connie's misery. "I should be doing that," she thought and began to tick off items on a list of her failings as a mother.

Still motionless and feeling exhausted, Connie noticed an all-too-familiar lump forming in her throat and tears welling in her eyes. She knew her day would go straight downhill. In a few minutes she would be staring at the clothes in her closet, hating every outfit she owned and hating herself for being "too fat to look good in anything." In a few hours she would be at her desk in the billing department of a local hospital listening to the other administrative assistants gossip and banter as if they hadn't a care in the world. She could even hear her own voice—shrill and impatient—demanding that they quiet down so she could concentrate on her work. Then, before the end of the day, she would do or say something to exasperate her husband and children. A disgusted look would pass from one to the other, and she would know they were thinking, "Pay no attention to Mom. She's in one of her moods again."

And of course Connie *was* in a mood, a blue mood. The same sort of gloomy, despondent mood that descends upon us all from time to time. No one is immune. When surveyed, most Americans say that they feel blue approximately five to ten days out of the year.

The hallmarks of a blue mood—sadness or irritability, self-pity, lethargy, a sense of helplessness or hopelessness that makes your life seem like purgatory and your future look bleaker still—are unpleasant but not necessarily debilitating, and they are generally short-lived. A typical case of the blues lasts a day, a week, maybe two.

Connie's case was not typical, however. When asked how long her blue moods lasted, she found the question absurd. It implied that the blues go away, and hers did not. The same achy, downbeat mood had greeted Connie nearly every morning and stayed throughout the day for the past five years.

JOEL'S STORY

Joel, a social studies teacher in his late twenties, knew all about the blues. He, too, had had them for years.

When I met him, Joel did not have the appetite he once had and was less interested in activities he once enjoyed. Although he felt content and self-confident for fleeting moments every now and then, he could not remember the last time an upbeat mood had lasted for more than a day or two.

"Nothing really gets through to me," he said. "Everything's very intellectual, very disconnected. I'll think, 'Now you're working,' 'Now you're eating dinner,' 'Now you're listening to music,' as if I were watching those things happen to someone else and doing a running commentary on them."

On the surface, Joel's life had changed very little since he arrived in San Francisco six years ago. "I still go to work every day," he said. "I still manage to make my classes interesting, supervise extracurricular activities, and let my students know I'm there to listen if they need to talk. But more and more I feel as if I'm just going through the motions, as if I'm walking around in a fog and not really experiencing life."

A talented musician, Joel used to look forward to the twice-weekly jam sessions at the jazz club around the corner from his home. "But now I practically have to force myself to go," he explained. "I still feel okay once I get there, but it takes a real effort and a major pep talk just to get myself out the door." And although Joel admitted that he felt lonely and isolated—as though everybody else is inside and he is at the plate-glass window looking in—not even a major pep talk could motivate him to go out and meet new people.

Prone to nostalgic reminiscing about the past, Joel sometimes wished he could return to the carefree life-style and easy camaraderie he experienced while in college. Back then he was happy-go-lucky and sure of himself. But he did not expect to ever feel that good again. Shrugging unenthusiastically, as if he had resigned himself to being blue for the rest of his days, Joel concluded, "You grow up. You slow down. You don't have stars in your eyes anymore. That's reality. That's the way things are."

For most of us, blue moods are an occasional and inevitable feature of living in an imperfect world. Day-to-day pressures, losses, setbacks, or disappointments take their toll, and it is not unusual to react to such circumstances by feeling as alienated and unmotivated as Joel. Some of us are prone to the blues when holidays roll around. Others are adversely affected by the sunless days of winter. Even the common cold or a bout of the flu can lower the spirits. But when our circumstances change, so do we. The fog lifts, and we feel like our old selves again.

For Joel, though, the blues are a permanent fixture. There is no apparent reason for his downbeat state of mind, no circumstance that he can say is maintaining it. "This *is* my self," he said. "This is the way I am."

Joel is not the only one who feels that way. He and Connie are not alone. Five million American men and women share their plight, and you may too. If Connie's and Joel's thoughts, feelings, and behaviors resemble your own, if you get down and find that nothing cheers you up for long, let me assure you that blue is not just the way you are. Nor is it the way you will always have to be. What you are experiencing is dysthymic disorder.

DANIELLE'S STORY

Danielle, a forty-year-old artist, insisted that she had always been blue, and she believed she would be blue forever.

"I can't remember ever being truly happy or at peace with myself," she said. "Even as a young child I felt as if I didn't fit in anywhere. I always thought that no matter how hard I tried, I would never really be good enough at anything I did. I've spent my entire life feeling not good enough, as if I was born with pieces missing, with handicaps I had to push myself to overcome, though in the end I would not overcome them."

Danielle's negative self-assessment would take most outside observers by surprise. After all, her paintings were exhibited in prestigious art galleries and sold well for high prices. She owned a huge loft apartment and studio in Manhattan, traveled extensively throughout the world, and had a full social calendar whenever she was in town. Danielle even had a love life; she had been involved with Greg, a pediatric surgeon, for the past two years. In spite of all evidence to the contrary, Danielle still felt like a failure. What's more, she lived in a constant state of dread and indecisiveness.

"None of my paintings ever feels finished," she commented. "I stare at them and wonder if I could somehow make them better. And I cannot pick the ones to exhibit. My agent has to come and take the ones *she* thinks are ready." Terrified of making mistakes, Danielle did not trust herself to make decisions, and the more successful she became, the more insecure she felt. She became more convinced that "one wrong move could mean losing everything," and sometimes she would pursue this line of thinking until she visualized herself homeless and destitute, begging for spare change from people who were once part of her social circle.

"But, it's not always that bad," Danielle admitted. She sometimes went for as long as a month without feeling "really down or completely disgusted" with herself. But the blues always returned and with them the anxiety, blinding headaches, heart palpitations, insomnia, and nightmares that had plagued her since childhood. Whenever Danielle felt as if she was drowning in a sea of self-hatred, she did anything she could to anesthetize the pain, including taking double doses of Valium and drinking heavily.

"I suppose I should try harder to improve my outlook, to shake these moods once and for all," Danielle said halfheartedly, "but I'm not sure I can. It's like changing your mind once you've stepped onto the 'down' escalator. You can turn around and try to climb back up, but between fighting the downward motion of the escalator and squeezing past all the people in your way, you're never going to make it to the top, so why bother?"

MISDIAGNOSES

Although DD did not appear in the American Psychiatric Association's *Diagnostic and Statistical Manual of Mental Disorders* (DSM-III) until

1980, it is not a new condition. Sufferers of long-lasting, low-grade forms of depression have been walking through the doors of doctors' offices for decades.

Many clinicians, particularly those trained in Freudian psychoanalysis, might conclude that Danielle had "depressive neurosis." From their perspective the roots of chronic blue moods were embedded in influences that dated as far back as infancy, and DD sufferers were unwittingly reenacting disappointments experienced early in life. The psychodynamic approach was costly in many ways, including time. What is more, this approach did not necessarily relieve the patient's symptoms. As one woman I interviewed put it, "After five years of analysis, I've gained plenty of insight into *why* I'm depressed. The problem is that I'm *still* depressed."

Fortunately, new research and the dramatic results of new forms of therapy prompted mental health professionals to rethink the problem and reclassify DD as a *mood disorder*. This reclassification brought with it a new perspective. Relatively mild but long-lasting depressions were no longer seen as signs of flawed characters or deep-seated neurosis but as a result of dysfunctional thoughts, feelings, or behavior, impaired relationships, or a biochemical imbalance—in the simplest of terms, a "glitch" somewhere in the system. The good news is that wherever that glitch may be, it can be fixed.

Although DD can be treated successfully, with noticeable improvement seen in a matter of weeks, it remains a mystery to most Americans—including medical and mental health professionals who are still in the process of learning about it. As a result, DD often goes unrecognized or undetected and can all too easily be overlooked, misdiagnosed, or mistreated.

MISTREATMENT

Many DD sufferers begin their quest for answers and relief by consulting a physician, a reasonable starting point, since a number of medical conditions and medications can have adverse effects on your mood. Unfortunately, many DD sufferers tell their doctors only about their physical symptoms and not their psychological ones. Connie, for instance, made numerous trips to her doctor's office in hopes of finding a cure for her chronic fatigue, back pain, sinus headaches, sore muscles, and a list of other maladies. She never mentioned her blue mood, and her doctor either did not detect it or did not consider it important. Connie was told there was nothing physically wrong with her, and she definitely did not like the insinuation that it was all in her head, that she was creating these ailments to get attention. She was not a hypochondriac. Regrettably, many DD sufferers are treated as if they are, and this adds to their sense of helplessness and hopelessness.

In addition, DD resembles and can be masked by other problems, making it extremely difficult to pin down—even for highly trained therapists. For instance, you will meet Andrea, a twenty-seven-year-old computer programmer who originally went into therapy after a series of disappointing relationships. "I have a problem with intimacy," she told her therapist. "My relationships hardly ever get off the ground, and even when they do, it's only a matter of time until they fall apart." Andrea had several other problems and many of the symptoms of DD, but she presented her "trouble with intimate relationships" as her main concern and rarely brought up anything else. "I learned a lot about myself," Andrea acknowledged, "and I learned about other things I could do, but I didn't do them. I thought it was just taking a long time for anything to sink in." Actually DD was getting in Andrea's way, preventing her from putting her newfound insight into action.

Similarly, Danielle, who had been in and out of therapy for years, had what is sometimes referred to as an "agitated" depression. Her insomnia, tension headaches, and tendency to get agitated whenever she was called upon to make a decision made her seem more anxious than depressed. She also used both tranquilizers and alcohol to excess. Although both her inability to manage anxiety and her substance abuse demanded attention, neither was the "real" source of distress.

When their initial efforts were unsuccessful, Andrea, Danielle, and Connie kept looking for answers. Eventually they found them and embarked upon the road to recovery. This makes them three of the fortunate few because, while DD is not all that difficult to overcome, the most common response to chronic cases of the blues is no response at all: Up to two-thirds of all DD sufferers do not seek help or otherwise take action on their own behalf.

The reason for this is that DD creeps up on you gradually. You lose your energy, enthusiasm, and positive outlook a little bit at a time, and although being blue day after day does not feel good, it may not feel bad enough to do anything about it. After a while being blue seems like your normal frame of mind, becoming a way of life, and you may not even be aware that you are depressed. As Joel put it, "People keep saying, 'You seem down. You're so withdrawn, so quiet. You're shutting out the world.' And you think, 'So what else is new?' You feel that there is nothing really wrong with you, or anything that anyone could do something about. What could you say to a therapist? 'Gee, the thrill is gone. Life isn't a laugh a minute'?"

SUFFERERS AND OTHER VICTIMS

When you and the people in your life, including the professionals whose help you seek, do not understand the problem and do not know about the effective measures for overcoming DD, the blues will *not* go away. Indeed, additional and more debilitating problems are likely to develop.

DD sufferers are apt to experience ever-increasing despair and discomfort. Overall functioning may decrease so that the sufferer accomplishes less and less and feels more and more inadequate as a result. The ability to cope with disappointment, losses, and stress may diminish, and anxiety, eating, and sleeping problems may become more pronounced. Even if they never become "clinically" depressed, they may wonder if life is worth living and think about suicide.

People with DD are prone to ingesting alcohol, illicit drugs, and over-the-counter or prescription sleeping pills. If they become dependent on these substances—as many dysthymics do—they further complicate their lives. In addition, DD sufferers spend countless sums seeking medical and psychological treatment that does not make them healthier.

If nothing else said thus far has convinced you to take your own or a loved one's chronically depressed condition seriously, this list of DD's potential repercussions should. The longer a chronic case of the blues continues, the more damage it does not only to DD sufferers themselves but to everyone around them as well.

L ike any spouse, relative, friend, or co-worker of someone with DD, Dan could not help but feel the impact of Connie's blue moods. The changes in his wife baffled him. They also placed a burden on him. Dan had assumed responsibility for many of the household chores that Connie, in her chronically fatigued condition, tended to neglect. He had abandoned vacation plans and turned down countless invitations because Connie "just didn't feel up to" traveling or socializing. "Connie's so cranky and miserable that it's tough for *me* to be around her," he said, "and it's even harder for the kids. I try to make it up to them, to spend time with them, help them with their homework, things like that." In the beginning Dan tried to be cheerful at all times for his children's sake and in the hope that it would affect Connie in a positive way. "But I just can't pull it off the way I used to," Dan admitted. In fact, Dan sometimes felt as exhausted and irritable as his wife. But mostly he felt sad: "I love Connie, and it hurts to see her this way all the time. I want her to be happy again. I want to help her, but I don't know what to do."

The people who have DD are not its only victims. With their pessimism, irritability, neediness, and negativity spreading outward like ripples in a pond, DD sufferers usually affect those around them by their blue mood. In turn, those affected react to the person whose blues won't go away, thereby perpetuating or exacerbating the problem. Under normal circumstances we would try to find professional help for a person who is suffering from a major depression, especially one who is talking about suicide and is no longer able to function on a daily basis. We would be concerned and do everything we can to ease the burden of someone who has suffered a loss or is going through a crisis. When someone is down in the dumps day in and day out for years, however, you don't know what to do.

Initially you sympathize and try to reassure and comfort the DD sufferer. You try to cheer him or her up, take the pressure off, give advice for solving a problem, offer to watch the kids, lend an ear if a listener is needed. You do your best to be supportive, to assure the depressed individual that you understand. And you do. At one time or another you have been blue yourself, but because your blues went away after a day or two, you assume that the DD sufferer's will, too. When they don't, when someone else's blues linger for weeks, months, or even years, your patience wears thin.

"I just don't see what she has to complain about," said Connie's older sister Pat. "She has a good marriage, a sweet husband—with the patience of a saint—two healthy kids, a nice house, a new car. We should all be so lucky. But does Connie feel that way? No. 'I'm tired,' she says.

'I'm fat. I'm bored. Nothing good ever happens to me.' And when it does, what does she say? 'It's a fluke. It won't last.'

"Look, I know life isn't a picnic, but you live it," Pat continued. "When you fall down, you pick yourself up, dust yourself off, and go on. But not Connie. She has taken up permanent residence in the pits and is dragging the rest of us down with her. Sometimes I get so frustrated that I could wring her neck. I just want to shake her and shout 'Snap out of it!' "

Rapidly reaching the end of your patience, you begin to cajole and harangue the DD sufferer. You repeatedly try to "shake some sense" into them, using everything from guilt ("The kids are worried sick about you") to threats ("If you think I'm going to sit around here just because you're depressed, you're crazy. I'll go out and find myself someone who knows how to have fun"). You begin to think of the DD sufferer as a whiner, a complainer, someone who gets some sort of morbid satisfaction out of being miserable. Rescinding your support altogether, you want to have nothing whatsoever to do with Ms. or Mr. Gloom and Doom. All of the above creates additional inner turmoil for both you and the person whose blues won't go away. The DD sufferer doesn't feel better and you feel worse, endlessly frustrated and also guilt-ridden for turning against or abandoning someone who is down.

If someone you are close to has a chronic case of the blues, you can feel as victimized by their depression as they do. Their downbeat mood can leave you feeling as disheartened, pessimistic, and powerless as they feel, or even angry and frustrated. At the very least, someone whose blues won't go away will baffle and bewilder you.

2

Diagnosing
Dysthymic
Disorder

I'm *not* depressed," Joel insisted. "And believe me, I know depression when I see it. My mother had it off and on for years." With that established, Joel proceeded to describe his mother's symptoms, which he had observed as a child as well as in recent years.

"She'd stay in her bedroom for days, sometimes weeks, sleeping fourteen and fifteen hours at a time," he explained. "She couldn't eat and she didn't bathe or fix her hair or take care of the house or us kids. She'd cry often, even sob uncontrollably, wring her hands, the whole bit."

When Joel's mother was depressed, she moved and talked in slow motion and claimed to feel utterly alone, like a stranger even to herself. As Joel put it, "She spoke so softly, you could barely hear her, and she looked as though someone had strapped a two-hundred-pound weight on her and she had the burden of the world on her shoulders."

Sliding deeper and deeper into her depression, Joel's mother would compose suicide notes, leaving them half-finished on the kitchen counter, the dining room table, or wherever she happened to be when she started writing them. "That's how we knew it was time for her to go to the hospital again," Joel said.

SIMILARITIES WITH MAJOR DEPRESSION

What Joel described was indeed depression—"clinical" or "major" depression, to be exact. The symptoms of major depression are dramatic and debilitating. They are often so painful and overpowering that the person stops functioning with any semblance of normalcy at all.

In contrast, now as an adult, Joel held down a job, took care of himself, interacted with other human beings, and even participated in outside activities such as jamming with fellow jazz musicians twice a week. He was not particularly enthusiastic about any of this, but he was at least going through the motions of a normal life. Furthermore, although Joel sometimes thought that life "wasn't worth the effort it takes to live it," he had never seriously considered suicide.

Joel saw the differences between his mother's condition and his own as proof that he was not depressed. "It's nothing, really, I'm just a little down in the dumps," Joel kept assuring me. But if I had taken him at his word, I would have been doing him a disservice.

Joel may not have been *as* depressed as his mother, but he was still depressed. His long-standing case of the blues did not prevent him from functioning on a daily basis, but it did keep him from functioning as well as he could and deriving pleasure and a sense of self-worth from what he accomplished. Enveloped in a cloud of negativity, he viewed countless endeavors as "just not worth pursuing," and when he did pursue something, he reported "sleepwalking through it like a programmed computer in a human body." Joel had DD. He was suffering from a chronic, low-grade depression, which was no more normal than having a constant low-grade fever.

It is important to understand that even though you may not have as many problems as someone with major depression and even though the problems you have are not as severe, a blue mood that won't go away is still serious. A chronic, low-grade depression is still depression; it still adversely effects the quality of your life.

In order to overcome DD you must first acknowledge that it is something to be overcome. You must realize that being blue is not just the way you are but is a sign that you are suffering from a legitimate and curable illness. What follows is a detailed portrait of this complex mood disorder.

While it is true that no one has *all* of its symptoms, it is helpful to know all of them in order to fully understand DD and its ramifications.

The Dominant Feature: Blues. Are you blue (down, out of sorts, sad, cranky) most of the day?

Do you feel that way more days than not?

Within the past two years, have the periods when you were free of the blues lasted no more than two months at a time?

People with DD answer yes to these three questions. They are blue most of the time, and their prevailing mood might best be described as gloomy, pessimistic, and joyless. Small frustrations and disappointments seem enormous and preoccupy their thoughts. If there is a negative way to look at an experience, they will find it.

Of course, no two cases of the blues are identical. While Connie was primarily irritable and whiny, Joel felt empty, disconnected, and unmotivated. Danielle was prone to worrying and stewing, berating herself over her perceived shortcomings, brooding about the past, and conjuring up worst-case scenarios for the future. Someone else may throw a neverending self-pity party, bemoaning his sad state of affairs and constantly reminding himself of his powerlessness to improve matters. But no matter what form the blue mood takes, being in one most of the time is a hallmark of DD.

Some DD sufferers are continuously down in the dumps with never a noticeable improvement. Others are intermittently blue with brief periods of normalcy. Although a case of the blues lasting eight or nine consecutive months could still be considered a problem, for a psychotherapist to diagnose a person as dysthymic, the "good" times must last for less than two months.

Six Specific Signs and Symptoms. The following are the symptoms of dysthymia listed as diagnostic criteria in the American Psychiatric Association's revised *Diagnostic and Statistical Manual of Mental Disorders* (DSM-III R). If two or more contain thoughts, feelings, or behaviors closely resembling your own, then you are a candidate for the dysthymic disorder diagnosis.

1. *Poor appetite or overeating.* The blues can depress your appetite as well as your mood, making food seem less appealing and hardly worth the effort required to purchase, prepare, or consume it. Even though eating may seem like a chore, however, you do not reduce your food intake drastically. And unlike clinically depressed individuals, you do not necessarily lose significant amounts of weight.

    Many DD sufferers find themselves eating more rather than less. Like a parent who tells her child to clean her room or there will be no ice cream for dessert or one who asks the child if she feels better as she wipes cookie crumbs from her tearstained face, you may comfort, bribe, or reward yourself with food. Or needing a quick energy boost, you may instinctively reach for anything containing sugar. DD sufferers often crave or binge on sweets and other junk foods.

2. *Sleep disturbances.* Mood disturbances such as DD cross the wires in your body's internal time clock, changing how or how much you sleep and throwing off the natural rhythms that keep you feeling healthy and refreshed. Sleep disturbances that go hand in hand with DD include hypersomnia (sleeping too much), insomnia (sleeping too little or having difficulty falling asleep), restless sleep (tossing, turning, perspiring, talking in your sleep), nightmares, or waking early and being unable to go back to sleep.

3. *Low energy and excessive tiredness.* Although you are not immobilized by lethargy the way people in a major depressive episode are, you are apt to feel fatigued and unmotivated. General aches and pains, stomach upsets, and other complaints that are not the result of a physical ailment can also be symptoms of a depressed emotional state.

4. *Difficulty in concentrating and/or making decisions.* When you have the blues, you may think in slow motion. You may have difficulty grasping concepts as quickly as you once did or be easily distracted and lose your train of thought in mid-sentence, or even appear wishy-washy.

5. *Low self-esteem.* You may have little confidence in your ability to

capture other people's interest. You might have an equally negative opinion of your appearance, your competence as an employee, or your overall worth as a person.

Awash in a sea of self-criticism, you may assume that other people share your opinion and therefore misconstrue even the most harmless comments, hearing put-downs and disapproval where none were intended. Or, as Danielle did, you may set perfectionist standards for yourself and then consider yourself a failure and hopelessly inept whenever you make even a small mistake.

Like many of the problems associated with DD, low self-esteem is caused by the blues but also maintains them. You think so little of yourself that you may not be sure you deserve to feel better, and you have so little confidence in your abilities that it is hard to believe your efforts to beat the blues could succeed. Consequently, you may give up too easily or not try at all.

6. *Feelings of hopelessness.* Under the influence of a chronic case of the blues, you may go from the premise that "life is hard" to the conclusion that it is "hardly worth living." There is no point in telling yourself that tomorrow could be better. From this pessimistic point of view, tomorrow seems likely to be every bit as bad as today— and maybe even worse. You may feel powerless to improve your circumstances or your mood.

OTHER COMPONENTS

The symptoms listed in the DSM-III R are not the only ones researchers and psychotherapists have observed in their dysthymic patients. The following cognitive, emotional feeling, and behavioral components are also quite prevalent.

LACKING INTEREST IN ANYTHING AMUSING OR FUN AND DERIVING LESS PLEASURE AND SATISFACTION FROM ACTIVITIES PREVIOUSLY CONSIDERED ENJOYABLE. In the throes of a blue mood that won't go away, things that once made you laugh no longer seem funny. Indeed, you may consider them trivial or dumb. Accomplishments that once gave you a sense of satisfaction no longer produce that effect. They seem hollow or as if they were happening to someone else. Pursuits that once delighted you are abandoned because they seem like unjustifiable extravagances or require more energy than you can summon. Psychologists refer to this unwillingness or impaired ability to experience pleasure as *anhedonia*. The word "joylessness" sums it up just as well.

Andrea, the twenty-seven-year-old computer programmer, had this symptom of DD. Friends and co-workers regularly invited her to go with them to museums, restaurants, concerts, and movies, but Andrea regularly turned them down, claiming to be too tired or simply not in the mood. She no longer took art or dance classes she once had enjoyed immensely and no longer went to garage sales and flea markets, a favorite pastime. Exhausted by the time the weekend rolled around, Andrea went to bed early and slept late, sometimes not even bothering to get dressed or leave her apartment. When she wasn't working or sleeping, Andrea was apt to be curled up on the sofa in front of the television with a supply of snack food.

As her blues took hold, Andrea, like many other DD sufferers, had stopped doing the things she enjoyed and had fallen into the habit of doing whatever seemed easiest. Without intending to develop it or realizing that she was doing it, Andrea was creating a life in which the opportunities to experience pleasure were few.

Of course, you can also *knowingly* root pleasure from your life as if it were an unsightly weed, thinking that you do not deserve it or fearing that making room in your life to experience it would only make things more unmanageable than they already are. Connie seemed to deliberately banish all opportunities to feel good. Thanks to her chronic case of the blues, there wasn't a single thing that she truly wanted to do, only things she had to do, or could not get out of doing. When anyone suggested a potentially uplifting or amusing activity to Connie, she invariably replied, "I don't have time. I have chores to do, errands to run. I'm already behind schedule, so I can't fritter away time like that."

Connie was not even excited by the all-expense-paid trip to the Bahamas that her husband's company gave him as a reward for work well done. Upon hearing about it, her first thoughts were: "So much to do. Find a sitter for the boys, get caught up around the house, make arrangements at work—I wish we didn't have to go at all."

While Joel continued to engage in pursuits he once found rewarding, he did not enjoy them as much or at all. "The thrill is gone," he quipped sardonically. Although more difficult to grasp than no longer doing the things you once enjoyed, doing the same things but feeling unenthusiastic, indeed completely unmoved by them, is also anhedonia.

BECOMING ANXIOUS AND FEARFUL ABOUT UPCOMING EVENTS, DREADING THE FUTURE, AND WORRYING ABOUT THINGS THAT MIGHT GO WRONG. Louise, a petite, high-strung woman in her late fifties, was a compulsive worrier in addition to being chronically depressed. Over the years, she and her husband, Jim, had weathered some lean times when the small grocery store they owned brought in barely enough money to make ends meet. But during the past decade their New England village had become a popular getaway spot for young urban professionals, and the store had consistently turned a tidy profit. Even so, Louise was convinced that she and Jim were in terrible financial shape and that in spite of all their hard work there would never be enough money for them to retire. Jim constantly assured Louise that they would not spend their old age in abject poverty, but she did not believe him. She always stayed behind after the store closed, going over the day's receipts, calculating and recalculating in order to figure out if she and Jim would have enough money to live comfortably fifteen years hence.

When she wasn't worrying about money, Louise worried about her health. Although a recent physical had netted her a clean bill of health, she was certain that catastrophe was just around the corner in the form of a terminal illness. As soon as she learned about any disease, she began looking for signs in herself. She was especially concerned about getting cancer and sometimes lay awake at night worrying about the malignant cells that might be silently growing somewhere within her.

This perpetual, unproductive worrying, when thoughts of potential disasters, past failures, and personal inadequacies remain fixed in your head, is called *rumination*. Troubling thoughts are examined from every angle until you spiral into the depths of despair or work yourself into a frenzy.

"It's like riding on a runaway train," said Danielle. "Once my mind gets going, there's no stopping it. Before I know it, I'm as wired as a wind-up toy. My heart is palpitating, my pulse is racing, my ears are ringing, and I feel as if my head is about to explode." Those physical sensations are all signs of anxiety, and according to Dr. James Kocsis of New York Hospital–Cornell Medical Center, 62 percent of the DD sufferers he surveyed reported problems with it.

Worrying is a universal pastime, and feeling anxious is an inevitable, inescapable occurrence in everyone's life. Both *can* be used to your advantage; anxiety, in particular, is the psyche's way of warning you of a real or imagined threat to your physical or emotional well-being. Anticipating negative outcomes works in your best interest when it prompts you to develop contingency plans for dealing with unpleasant events (or your feelings about them) should they occur. But if you are a DD sufferer who ruminates the way Louise and Danielle do, then you may not see or consider your options. Convinced of your own powerlessness, you are prone to do nothing about the concerns that preoccupy you except become more preoccupied with them.

BEING LESS PRODUCTIVE THAN YOU ONCE WERE, REQUIRING MUCH MORE TIME TO COMPLETE EVEN ROUTINE TASKS, LOSING INTEREST QUICKLY, AND PROCRASTINATING OR ABANDONING EFFORTS SOON AFTER THEY ARE INITIATED. Dr. Kocsis reports that 57 percent of DD sufferers are not as productive as they were in the past. Other DD symptoms, including chronic fatigue, lack of self-confidence, and difficulty concentrating, are partially to blame, and so are the apathy and boredom that go hand in hand with any blue mood. Few projects seem worth the time and energy they consume, and the routine tasks of daily living—grooming, laundry, cooking, housekeeping, and so on— may seem so dull and draining that you literally have to badger yourself into doing them. Worse yet, DD robs you of your sense of accomplishment. No matter what you do or how much progress you make toward a goal, you tell yourself that you should have done it sooner, could have done it better, or will only have to do it over again tomorrow.

FEELING THAT NO ONE VALUES YOUR OPINION OR THAT EVERYONE EXPECTS TOO MUCH FROM YOU, AND WISHING THAT OTHERS WOULD DO WHAT YOU ASK OR LET YOU SAY NO WITHOUT HASSLING YOU OR MAKING YOU FEEL GUILTY. If you lack assertiveness skills and hold little hope for success to begin with, you may have trouble asking for assistance or saying no to other people's requests, no matter how unreasonable they may be. Or you may go to the opposite extreme and make some rather unreasonable demands yourself. Then again, you may rely on manipulation: In order to get something you want or get out of something you would prefer not to do, you may use your depressed state to elicit sympathy or induce guilt—a ploy that can work in the short term, but ultimately backfires.

This symptom, which more than 50 percent of the DD sufferers cited in Kocsis's article had, is primarily the result of not knowing *how* to get what you want. The logical conclusion is that you need to learn effectiveness skills, but a blue mood is liable to prevent you from drawing this conclusion and instead lead you to believe that failure and disappointment are your destiny.

ATTRIBUTING YOUR CIRCUMSTANCES AND EMOTIONAL STATE TO FATE, LUCK, OR CHANCE. Whether you think of it as fate, rotten luck, or your cross to bear, you may hold forces beyond your control responsible for anything and everything you experience. This is called being externally focused. Some DD sufferers think they exert no influence on their own lives at all. Others attribute only positive occurrences to chance, luck, or fate and automatically blame themselves when things go wrong. If you fall into that category, you may find yourself apologizing for circumstances that truly are beyond your control. ("I'm sorry about the traffic. I should have known this would happen," you say even though there was no way you could have known that a tractor trailer would overturn.)

HAVING DIFFICULTY GETTING TO KNOW OR GETTING ALONG WITH PEOPLE. Chronic depression can make you chronically shy and introverted. It can prompt you to withdraw from friends and social activities. It can even be the major factor behind a perplexing series of disappointing romantic relationships or the conflicts in your marriage. Clearly, this symptom covers a lot of ground. How and how often you interact with other people may become less satisfying than it used to be, more anxiety-provoking than you would like it to be, or a constant source of confusion.

IT MAY NOT BE DD

People who are grieving over a recent loss or who are reacting to a life crisis, and all those who come down with an everyday, run-of-the-mill case of the blues, will have symptoms almost identical to those described above.

Normal blues are transient, however. In contrast, DD goes on and on. In one recent research study, close to half of the dysthymic subjects said they had been blue for more than ten years.

Of course, no one is upbeat all of the time. In fact, feeling blue or being down in the dumps is an understandable and appropriate reaction when you encounter trying circumstances and unsettling events. For instance, if you are passed over for a promotion, it is natural to feel disheartened, to question your competence and even to go over your job performance with a fine-tooth comb looking for areas where you failed to measure up to your own or other people's standards. But you would not be in that same blue mood two years later, nor would you think of yourself as a complete failure or conclude that you will never get what you want out of life, as many DD sufferers do. The chronic blues that characterize DD are out of proportion to reality and spill over into all areas of your life, painting everything with the same bleak brush.

It is also natural to feel sad or grief-stricken over the death of a loved one, the breakup of a marriage or long-term relationship, being robbed, declaring bankruptcy, or any other loss. Indeed, under such circumstances and during any life crisis, sadness and grief are not only inescapable but also serve a purpose; they are part of a healing process that enables you to finish one chapter of your life and move on to the next. And you do move on. No matter how great the loss or how serious the setback, as time passes, your grief and sorrow diminish and you get on with your life. DD sufferers do not. They get stuck in the quicksand of their own despair without really knowing how they got bogged down in the first place.

Take Connie, for example. At twenty, she was an adventurous, fun-loving young woman with a seemingly limitless supply of energy. She was a real go-getter and had all sorts of plans for the future. She wanted to do a million things, and others never doubted she would do them. She was the ultimate positive thinker. She never let anything get in her way.

At twenty-two Connie met Dan, and he recalls that she could "waltz into a room and dazzle everybody in it. She bubbled over with joy and optimism." Throughout their courtship, during the early years of their marriage, and even after a miscarriage at age twenty-four, Connie retained her positive outlook. According to Dan, no matter what happened, Connie could find the humor in it and turned ordinary, everyday events into three-ring-circus productions.

At twenty-seven she slowed down a bit, but with two babies to care for, that was understandable. "Even then," Dan said, "it was nothing for Connie to pack up the car on a moment's notice so we could spend a day at the beach or the weekend at my parents' cabin in the mountains."

Then, beginning sometime after her twenty-eighth birthday and happening so gradually that no one, not even Connie herself, noticed, she changed. By the time she was thirty-four she was dragging herself through life as if it were a jail sentence. "I don't know what did it," Dan said. "But if you hadn't seen Connie in the last five years and saw her today, you wouldn't believe she was the same person."

Connie did not know either. Her life-style was neither trying nor traumatic. Nothing posed a noticeable threat to her well-being. "I really don't have any reason to feel the way I do," Connie said with a sigh.

Dan and Connie just described one of the most baffling aspects of DD: its insidious onset. The blues creep up on you slowly and for reasons that are not apparent to you. You do not realize that the clinging vine of chronic depression has taken root until you are already entangled in it. You try to trace its origins but are unable to pinpoint when your blue mood began or what might have triggered it. Sometimes there were problems in the distant past—a job loss, rocky relationships, difficulty adjusting to life in a new city, or a health problem. But DD sufferers invariably believe that they got over that hurdle years ago. For others there appears to have been no hurdle at all. None can say with any certainty what keeps them down in the dumps, but they stay there for at least two years if they are dysthymic.

Certain medical problems as well as a number of other psychological disorders can cause depressionlike symptoms or resemble DD in many ways. Consequently, before deciding that you definitely have DD, a psychiatrist or psychotherapist would attempt to eliminate any other condition that might be the source of your distress by asking questions to ascertain whether the following conditions exist:

A MEDICAL PROBLEM OR DEPRESSION TO WHICH PRESCRIPTION MEDICATIONS ARE CONTRIBUTING. Candace, a bright, high-achieving senior in college, recently discovered that medical problems can bring on psychological ones, including chronic cases of the blues. She almost flunked out of school because of mysterious, unrelenting depressions that made it all but impossible for her to concentrate. At first she and others close to her assumed her problems were "all in her head." But they were not. In fact, the real culprits were her body and a medical condition called *hypothyroidism*. If you have this or another glandular problem, a vitamin or mineral deficiency, hepatitis, multiple sclerosis, lupus, or certain types of cancer, it could be the source of your long-lasting blue mood. Proper treatment for your physical ailment should relieve your depressionlike symptoms as well.

In some instances, of course, the treatment is the problem. All medications have side effects, and some of the most common ones—lethargy, sleep and appetite disturbances, irritability—are virtually identical to the symptoms of DD. A retired executive in his sixties found that out when, soon after being treated for high blood pressure, he began feeling blue and lost interest in almost everything he once enjoyed, including sex. Unwilling to spend his golden years feeling depressed, Paul marched right back into his doctor's office and registered a complaint. Once his blood pressure medicine was changed, Paul felt like his old self again.

In addition to antihypertensives, drugs used to treat Parkinson's disease, tuberculosis, and cancer as well as certain hormones and steroids, can produce depressive symptoms. If you suspect that either a medical condition or the medication being used to treat it is contributing to your depressed state of mind, consult your physician.

A MAJOR DEPRESSION BEING EXPERIENCED NOW OR WITHIN THE LAST SIX MONTHS. As Joel's description of his mother's suffering revealed, a major depressive episode involves symptoms that are more severe and debilitating than those which DD sufferers experience. When the disorder is at its worst, you cannot function at work, within your family, or in your social group. Your feelings of worthlessness and despair can become so overblown that you seriously consider suicide as a way out.

If you are *that* depressed, please seek professional help immediately. If someone you know is that depressed and especially if he is fantasizing or talking about suicide, obtain help for him. It is a common and tragic fallacy that people who threaten suicide do not go through with it. They do.

Three years ago, Simone, a forty-two-year-old paralegal, was that depressed. After receiving treatment for her major depressive episode, she reported that she was "completely back to normal." But several months after completing treatment, she noticed that she was having a hard time concentrating on her work, was no longer sleeping soundly through the night, and felt tired throughout the day. Although Simone knew that these symptoms were minor compared to the way she felt while in the throes of major depression, it dawned on her that "things just weren't quite right." And indeed they were not.

Like an estimated 20 percent of all people who experience major depressive episodes, Simone had made an *incomplete recovery*. She inadvertently traded her debilitating symptoms for more bearable but longer-lasting ones. If you were clinically depressed less than six months prior to developing your chronic case of the blues, then you may have done so, too.

EXTREME OR MILD BUT NOTICEABLE MOOD SWINGS. If you have DD, your mood rarely fluctuates, but when it does lift, you simply feel normal. If you swing back and forth between feeling depressed and feeling elated or euphoric, you may be suffering from *bipolar disorder* or its close but less debilitating "relative"—*cyclothymia*.

Bipolar disorder—more popularly known as manic depression—involves wide-ranging mood cycles. At one extreme are major depressive episodes like those described earlier. At the other extreme are periods of mania during which you might feel on top of the world and as if there is nothing you cannot do. You become extremely active, hardly sleep at all, and may even have grandiose delusions or hallucinate. During a manic phase you are apt to be jittery: Your thoughts race, you cannot sit still, you talk incessantly. Because your illness has impaired your judgment, you make decisions that seem odd to others and engage in behaviors that seem reprehensible to them—promiscuous or unsafe sexual activity, for instance, or squandering large amounts of money.

Michele, the manager of a retail clothing store, had what might be considered a mild version of bipolar disorder. Her mood cycled between highs and lows, but neither were as intense as the manic and depressive episodes just described. When she was up, Michele sailed through life without a hitch. Nothing—not her customers, her suppliers, her noisy neighbors, or reminders of her recent divorce—seemed to bother her. She had energy to spare and took on numerous commitments. But eventually Michele's abundant energy and positive outlook deserted her. When she was down, everything irritated her, projects embarked upon with gusto only weeks earlier were abandoned, routine tasks went undone, memories of the divorce haunted her, and she spent hours ruminating about why her marriage failed.

Michele's noticeable yet far from incapacitating mood swings are signs of cyclothymia. Cyclothymia is to bipolar disorder what dysthymia is to major depression. Its symptoms are similar but less severe, and though they are distressing, you can continue to function on a day-to-day basis. Because the down stage of cyclothymia looks so much like DD, the two disorders are easily confused.

OTHER MENTAL DISORDERS. Jill had been blue most of the day more days than not for quite some time. She felt trapped, hopeless, and "out of touch with life." She was also afraid to leave her house. The mere thought of walking to the end of her own driveway filled her with dread, reminding her of previous outings when she had experienced chest pain, shortness of breath, profuse sweating, and the sense that she was dying. Because she was terrified of having another attack, Jill had stopped going shopping, meeting her husband for lunch, picking up her children from school, or doing anything else that took her more than a few blocks from her home.

Although Jill's depressive symptoms made it appear that she had DD, her "attacks," her overpowering fear that they would recur, and her voluntary imprisonment within the well-defined boundaries of safety she had set for herself all indicated that she had another psychiatric condition—panic disorder with agoraphobia.

Similarly, Robert started feeling blue when he lost his job as a highly paid personnel officer. Although he had considered himself quite good at what he did and initially felt optimistic about getting another position, actually landing a new job took longer than Robert expected. After dozens of interviews, he began to doubt that he would ever find another job. At one point he became so disheartened that he gave up the search completely. Eventually he settled for a position that was beneath both his capabilities and his salary requirements. This did nothing to lift his blue mood.

Had it persisted, Robert's lingering case of the blues could have evolved into DD, but within six months his optimism and self-confidence returned. Robert's gloomy mood lifted, and he renewed his job search, ultimately landing an excellent position with a Fortune 500 company. He had been suffering from an adjustment disorder—an overreaction to an ordinary, albeit unpleasant, aspect of everyday living.

IT MAY BE DD WITH ANOTHER DISORDER

You can have another condition *and* a chronic low-grade depression at the same time. Clinicians who treat chronically depressed patients claim that they rarely see a "pure" case of DD, and an NIMH demographic study revealed that more than 75 percent of DD sufferers had other disorders as well. Perhaps the most common combination is DD and alcohol or drug abuse.

As you may recall, Danielle anesthetized the pain of chronic depression and "calmed her nerves" after a bout of anxious ruminating by taking double or triple the prescribed dosage of Valium, or drinking to excess. She developed an addiction to both tranquilizers and alcohol as a result of the dysthymia that existed *prior to* the substance abuse.

Conversely, Maury, a real estate agent, developed a chronic case of the blues as a result of his alcoholism. For years he had boosted his self-confidence, revved himself up to make a sales pitch, made social situations less nerve-racking and life in general more palatable by having a few drinks at lunch, a few more with dinner, and so on right up until bedtime. Although he acknowledged this behavior, Maury did not consider it a problem. His problem, he claimed, was "not being able to shake this depression. I've had it for couple of years now, and it seems to be getting worse." Alcohol, which had seemed to improve Maury's frame of mind in the past, no longer had an uplifting effect. If anything, he became more depressed while drinking than on the morning after when he was hung over.

This outcome was inevitable. Because alcohol reduces or removes your inhibitions, under its influence you act as if you hadn't a care in the world. But the fact of the matter is that alcohol as well as a number of other seemingly mood-elevating substances have a depressive effect on your brain and body. Over an extended period of time it is that effect which lingers and not the false sense of gaiety and self-confidence. Moreover, substance abuse eventually leads to a series of life failures— lost jobs, broken relationships, financial problems, and the like—which also can set off and maintain a chronic case of the blues.

DD can also be secondary to other psychological problems, especially those that keep people socially isolated the way Jill's panic disorder did. Panic attacks, phobias, obsessions and compulsions, paranoia, and so on, impair your ability to move around freely and interact with other people, limiting your opportunities to feel pleasure or be productive and virtually guaranteeing that you will feel depressed. As your primary disorder persists, so do your depressive symptoms, and they can evolve into DD. For similar reasons, DD commonly occurs in conjunction with primarily physical conditions as well—most notably those that involve disfigurement, disabilities, and chronic pain.

The overlap between dysthymia and major depression is considerable. When both occur simultaneously, psychiatrists diagnose a *double depression*. DD is considered the primary problem if there was no major depressive episode during the first two years you were blue and none during the six months prior to the onset of your blues. Otherwise, it is secondary to the major depressive disorder.

YOUR FIRST STEP TOWARD RECOVERY
At this point you may be thinking, "Now I'm really depressed." Taking a cold, hard look at your blue thoughts, feelings, and behaviors often has that effect. Indeed, reading about the symptoms of DD may have led you to believe that you are worse off than you thought and that you will never dig yourself out of the deep hole you are in. Or, you may feel that only a real idiot (loser, incompetent fool) could have made such a complete mess of his life and that you probably deserve everything you're getting. You might also believe it will take years to get better or that you'll never make it.

Drawing such unsavory conclusions is to be expected. No matter how you look at it, acknowledging the havoc that DD has wreaked on your life is not easy. However, getting more depressed or concluding that you deserve to stay down in the dumps is the worst possible way to look at the situation. If you continue to think that way, you will not find out how you can get better. If you don't already have one, stop now and purchase a notebook. Open to a fresh page and copy the following statements onto it:

1. My blue thoughts, feelings, and behaviors are not irreversible character flaws. They are symptoms of a treatable illness. People can and do recover from DD.
2. What's done is done. I cannot go back and change the past; however, I can learn how to do things differently in the future.
3. Other people are in this predicament. They have a problem, but they also have skills, strengths, talents, and other positive attributes. So do I.
4. As painful as it may feel right now, by recognizing, coming to understand, and acknowledging the problems that chronic blues have caused me, I am taking a step in the right direction—my first step toward recovery.

After you have written these statements, read them to yourself and then aloud. Then read them aloud again with more conviction. They are facts that contradict the inaccurate and unproductive ideas that ran through your mind earlier and that will probably arise again. Return to them as often as you need to. By writing and rewriting, then reading and rereading those facts, you neutralize your discouraging thoughts and become more open to the information you will need in order to overcome DD.

3

Why You Are
Susceptible

D anielle locked herself in the bathroom and turned the sink faucets on
full force so that her agent waiting outside might not hear her crying.
She did not want to explain her tears; she had no explanation for them.

"I should have been on top of the world," she said. An important
exhibition of Danielle's paintings was less than two months away, the
gallery owner was "practically gushing" praise for the work he had seen
thus far, and the brochure publicizing the show looked terrific. Danielle

29

had even been interviewed for the cover story of her alma mater's alumni magazine. "One of those 'former student makes good' pieces," Danielle commented. "It sort of made things official. I had arrived. I was a success." But Danielle did not feel successful. She felt depressed.

"I was crying my eyes out and coming apart at the seams." Danielle continued. "It didn't make sense."

Blues that won't go away rarely "make sense" to the people who have them or to anyone else. With logical explanations nowhere to be found, you begin grasping at straws. There has to be a reason, you think, and you conjure up possibilities that make at least some sense to you.

Fear of success, Danielle's agent thought. She felt that Danielle's panicky feeling was the result of her having everything she ever wanted within her grasp and that it suddenly dawned on her that it might not be as great as she imagined it would be. A friend of Danielle's thought it had to be something that happened to her as a child. Perhaps it was something traumatic, something buried deep in her subconscious.

Greg, Danielle's boyfriend, thought there was a much simpler explanation: She was just plain spoiled. He felt she pampered herself too much and had no concept of real suffering.

Theorizing and blaming the victim are common ways in which those close to someone with DD respond. Similar theories come to the minds of those down in the dumps. Despite their claim that blue is "just the way they are," DD sufferers try to figure out why. Indeed, they may become obsessively introspective as they probe deeper and deeper inside themselves for the source of their distress. Or they may turn their gaze outward, constantly comparing themselves to "normal" people and wishing they could be "normal," too.

Matthew, a fifty-year-old accountant who consulted numerous experts in hopes of "fixing" a problem no one could explain, had stopped looking for relief quite some time ago, but he still wanted some answers, especially when his friend Jerry was around.

Although Jerry was seven years older than Matthew, he seemed to have more energy than most men half his age. Jerry coached a softball team, played tennis three or four times a week, and went away on his boat whenever possible. Jerry and his wife still went out dancing, and they were known for the elaborate backyard barbecues they held throughout the summer. Just thinking about the preparation that went into those affairs exhausted Matthew. Indeed, Jerry's entire life-style left Matthew feeling tired. "I could never keep up that pace," he said, his voice tinged with envy.

In Jerry, Matthew saw everything that he himself was not, and Jerry's apparent happiness was a bitter pill to swallow. "Why can't I be that way?" Matthew wondered. "Why am I the one who ended up with the dreary, boring existence?" Looking beseechingly upward he asked, "Why me? What did I do to deserve such a drab, meaningless life? Why won't my blues go away?" The questions associated with DD are numerous and mind-boggling.

INHERITANCE FACTORS

For decades, research scientists have been searching for "agent blue"— a readily identifiable biological, social, or environmental factor that causes mood disorders such as DD. They have discovered not one answer but many, and it is quite likely that even more factors will be discovered as additional research is conducted. Furthermore, no clear-cut cause-and-effect relationships have been established. Although there is ample evidence that a combination of biological and psychological influences makes some people more susceptible to DD than others, the presence of any or even all of those influences does not guarantee that you will get DD. Likewise, the absence of those factors does not mean that you will never experience it.

This may disappoint those of you who think that there has to be a logical reason for your own unhappiness and that you have to find that reason before you can make the blues go away. The belief that problems cannot be solved until you figure out what caused them is a universal one, but it is not always accurate. You do not need to know exactly what brought on the blues in order to overcome them. What's more, just knowing that there are reasons for chronic blue moods and that they might be the reasons you suffer from them can be quite a relief— especially when you realize that you may have been "set up" for the blues long before you actually got them.

Nearly all clinical researchers agree on one point: The seeds of DD are sown in the past; in fact, they may have been planted before you were born. Mood disorders like DD are intergenerational illnesses: They run in the family. If you suspect you are a sufferer, it would be useful to find out whether any of your relatives suffered from chronic depressions.

Of the DD sufferers introduced thus far, Joel, Andrea, Matthew, and Louise had several relatives with mood disorders. Five of Joel's relatives (his mother, two of her sisters, his paternal grandmother, and his oldest brother) had experienced some form of depression at some time in their lives. In addition, Matthew and Andrea had parents with chronic depressions that were very similar or slightly more severe than their own. These are considered to be the two most powerful signs that someone will be susceptible to DD.

Other Traits of Families with Histories of Depression. If three or more of your relatives have had mood disorders, your family is said to be "loaded" with depression, and you have identified the first reason that you are prone to the blues: You are genetically vulnerable to them.

Although researchers have not isolated a specific "depression gene," there is ample evidence that the tendency to become depressed is indeed inherited. Some of that evidence has been gathered by studying identical twins with family histories of depression. Such research has revealed that in approximately two-thirds of the pairs studied, both twins developed depressive disorders even though they were raised apart.

But what about the other thirds, you may wonder. If mood disorders are inherited, why didn't they get one? The answer is that the illness itself is not inherited. Instead, a *predisposition* to the illness is passed from one generation to the next. When other contributing factors are present, you are more likely to develop DD than someone with different genetic material.

Your susceptibility to DD is substantially higher if either one or both of your parents were hospitalized for depression or committed suicide. In addition, research has shown that the younger someone was when a parent experienced a major depressive episode, the more likely it is that person will develop a mood disorder. These findings suggest that both nature (genetic vulnerability) *and* nurture (the environment in which you were raised) do their part to leave you prone to blue moods. Being exposed to depressed parents amplifies your inherited tendency to become depressed. In fact, many clinicians believe that because children of depressed parents often lead turbulent, unstable home lives and have their basic needs met inconsistently at best, they quite literally learn to be blue.

DEVELOPMENTAL FACTORS

Even very young children are astute observers of human nature. Their minds constantly absorb and process information from the world around them. In time, the information they have gathered forms a cohesive world view, giving them a sense of who they are, what is expected of them, and how other people are likely to respond. If all goes well, children develop a set of attitudes and beliefs that will serve them well throughout their lives: that they are valued and accepted despite their shortcomings; that hard work usually brings rewards; that they can influence the outcome of many situations; that they can get what they want or need out of life. Regrettably, when you grow up with a depressed parent, those are not the lessons you learn.

As you may recall from the last chapter, Joel's mother periodically slid into major depressive episodes and eventually was hospitalized because of them. The first time this happened, Joel was only two, and although he had no recollections of the episode, it undoubtedly had an impact on him. He still depended on his mother to feed him when he was hungry, comfort him when he was frightened, and be emotionally available to him when he needed to be reassured that he was safe, secure, and loved. With this in mind, you can imagine the terror he felt when he approached his severely depressed mother and she did not respond, or when she drove off with his father and did not return.

Joel was seven the next time his mother "slipped away." He recalled that "at first she just seemed distracted. When you talked to her, she'd be looking right at you but wouldn't hear a word you said. It felt really weird, as if you were invisible or something." Soon Joel's mother stopped paying attention to him at all. He and his sister and brothers had to fend for themselves, eating cheese sandwiches for dinner and wearing clothes that were washed but not ironed. "We could stay up as late as we wanted," he continued. "Not go to school if we didn't feel like it. And the whole time my dad acted as if there was nothing wrong. He just tuned everything out. It was as if he was waiting for something to tell him he had to move, he couldn't put it off any longer." When that moment arrived, Joel's father announced that he was taking his wife to the hospital.

By the time his mother had her third major depressive episode, Joel, who was thirteen, "knew the routine" and fell right into it. "Mom got depressed," he explained matter-of-factly, "things fell apart, and you rode out the storm and eventually things got better. End of story."

But of course the story did not end there. The lessons Joel had learned in the past became the basis for his behavior in the present and his predictions for the future.

Joel was convinced that reality wasn't supposed to be a laugh a minute. In fact, he felt, there wasn't much to laugh at or smile about at all. Joel thought life was *supposed to be* a "joyless struggle." Where did he get that idea? From his youthful observations of the two most influential people in his life: his parents.

Although Joel was lonely, he rarely left the confines of his apartment in order to meet new people, including women with whom he might forge a romantic relationship. However, when he did get out, the thought that motivated him was, "Okay, now you have to move. You can't put it off any longer," which was precisely the attitude he described his father as having.

Once he was on his way to a singles bar or social function, Joel conjured up worst-case scenarios: "If I see an attractive woman and try to catch her eye, she won't notice me. If I get up enough courage to talk to her, she'll look annoyed and turn away, or pretend to listen and *then* turn away, like I was invisible or something." This image—which matched the response he got from his mother when she was depressed—prevented Joel from initiating conversations with women who actually might have been quite receptive to him.

DYSFUNCTIONAL FAMILY FACTORS
Theresa, thirty-two, a salesclerk in a health-food store, has a fragile, waiflike quality that tugs at your heartstrings and compels you to reach out to her. You want to take her under your wing, and she lets you do

just that. "Other people have always made my decisions for me," Theresa said. "They're better at it than I am."

Theresa goes whichever way the wind blows, doing what is easiest, safest, and least likely to draw attention to her. At various times in her life she was going to be a writer of children's books, a nursery school teacher, a massage therapist, and a travel agent, but she quickly lost interest in each newly chosen career. Theresa went to college but did not get a degree. Taking fewer and fewer courses each semester and finally ceasing to register at all, Theresa drifted away from school and has been drifting ever since. She has lived in twelve cities in as many years and has been in a seemingly endless series of ill-fated romances. Believing that any man who shows an interest in her must be the soulmate who will finally give meaning and purpose to her life, Theresa "loses herself" in her relationships, "suffers horribly" when they end, and then starts the entire process all over again. Considering all this, it should come as no surprise that Theresa is chronically depressed.

Although two of Theresa's sisters are also depressed, mood disorders do not appear in previous generations of her family, and neither of Theresa's parents suffered from them. "My father was an alcoholic," she said tentatively. "Could that be why I'm depressed?" Yes, it could.

Long before the current proliferation of literature on Adult Children of Alcoholics (ACOAs), research on depression had revealed that children raised by alcoholic parents and especially daughters of alcoholic fathers ran an extremely high risk of becoming depressed adults. Many mental health practitioners report that both men and women whose parents were drug addicted or engaged in compulsive behavior (overeating, gambling, having affairs, and so forth) run similar risks, and the susceptibility to mood disorders is even greater when both parents had problems of that nature. From all indications the interpersonal upheaval of living in what is now called a dysfunctional family—one that fails to provide the basic nurturing of its children—is the contributing factor, and not the dysfunction itself.

A dysfunctional family is confusing, inconsistent, and unpredictable because everything in the household revolves around a parent's alcoholism, addiction, compulsive behavior, or some other dysfunction; parents are emotionally unavailable to their children, being too overwhelmed and distracted by their own problems to meet their youngsters' needs; family members routinely break promises and fail to communicate with one another, as well as lie and cover up for the dysfunctional member; there are rigid, unspoken rules that may make little sense but which everyone knows are never to be broken, and those rules prohibit the open expression of feelings and direct discussion of personal or family problems. If your family fits this description, you may have pretended that the problems in your home did not exist or did not bother you. Yet, because of them, you stopped trusting people and became dishonest, tuned out your true feelings, stifled your real self, and developed habits that you would carry with you for years to come.

Like millions of other children from dysfunctional families, you may have taken on a rigidly defined role instead of developing a multifaceted, independent identity. Perhaps you played the family "hero" who assumed responsibility for taking care of all of the problems in your family and keeping everything running smoothly. Or you may have been the family "scapegoat" who got into trouble and thus "took the heat off" the truly troubled family member. If you were the family "mascot," you reduced the tension in your household by distracting and entertaining everyone around you. Or like Theresa, you may have turned into a "lost child."

The fourth of seven children, Theresa described herself as "not the oldest or the youngest. Not the cutest or the smartest. Not even the brattiest. There was nothing special about me. I was just there." And she was plagued by a sense that she should not be. Theresa remembered many a night when she hid in her bedroom closet and wished that she had never been born. Somewhere along the line she had gotten the idea that she was the "burden" her father railed against during his drunken tirades. If she did not exist, her father would not be the way he was, she thought, and she tried to keep his awareness of her existence to a bare minimum. "I tried to fade into the woodwork," Theresa continued, "to stay out of the way."

Believing that "no one could be upset with me if they didn't notice me," Theresa withdrew into a fantasy world, keeping other family members at a distance and communicating with them as little as possible. She tried to make herself invisible and apparently succeeded. "Everyone was always forgetting about me," she claimed. "One year they forgot my birthday." And on a few occasions she was left behind at restaurants. While she was in the restroom, her family had piled into the car and driven away, unaware that she was not with them.

By "fading into the woodwork" Theresa was instinctively doing what she needed to do to survive in her dysfunctional family. By staying out of the way and never offering her opinion, making a decision, or letting anyone know how she felt, she created some semblance of safety and consistency in an environment that was patently unsafe and inconsistent. Every child in a dysfunctional home does this. Each in his or her own way plays a part and rarely deviates from it because to do so might destroy the delicate balance of a system that the child intuitively knows could explode at any minute. Within that system the strategy worked and the child survived.

Unfortunately, the behavior that enables you to adapt to a dysfunctional family becomes a deeply ingrained habit that you carry with you into adulthood. And as you can clearly see from Theresa's story, that behavior stops working to your advantage. Rather than protecting you from harm as it once did, your habitual behavior becomes self-defeating and can lead to a chronic case of the blues. This seems most likely to happen to "lost children," but family "heroes" run a close second. Having assigned themselves the task of making their dysfunctional family function normally, they are destined to fail, try harder, and fail again—a depressing pattern if ever there was one.

If your family was dysfunctional, you'd think you would know it, but you might not. Your need to feel safe and secure may have been so powerful that you believed the pretense that nothing was wrong. Or the dysfunction, which runs in families the way mood disorders do, may have skipped a generation. You have the interpersonal upheaval but nothing to pin it on. Or because the problem was not alcoholism, you did not see it as a sign of family dysfunction. Whether you knew about or previously overlooked the dysfunctional behavior going on around you, take some time now to think about any relatives who may have engaged in addictive or compulsive behaviors, including alcoholism, drug abuse, compulsive eating, workaholism, gambling, sex addiction, overspending, or people-pleasing.

LOSS AND CONFLICT FACTORS

Various researchers and practitioners have noted that a significant number of DD sufferers report that before they turned fifteen their parents had separated or divorced, a parent had abandoned the family, or one or both parents had died. In addition, in numbers great enough to notice, DD sufferers were born out of wedlock and had never known one of their parents, had been adopted, or had grown up in foster homes or orphanages. Psychologists call these kinds of childhood experiences "developmental object losses." If you suffered one, a connection you needed to feel safe, secure, or worthwhile was broken at a crucial time in your life. As a result, you may be plagued constantly by the fear of abandonment or rejection and have a powerful need to please or obtain approval.

Another trait shared by individuals with chronic cases of the blues is a strong desire to avoid conflict. People with this trait frequently report that within their families, conflicts were mishandled. Generally, one parent overreacted, becoming explosive, aggressive, or even violent. The other parent underreacted and appeared to be helpless, ineffective, or manipulative—things the DD sufferer would one day appear to be as well.

Chances are that by now you have identified at least one and perhaps several factors that may have contributed to your long-lasting blue mood. If you have not, there is still one more stone from the past to be turned. Underneath it you may find that the messages you received during childhood, even though well intentioned, may have prepared you for a chronic case of the blues.

Although there was no depression, obvious dysfunction, developmental object loss, or serious conflicts evident in Danielle's family, her blues also had their roots in the past. They could be traced to the relationship between Danielle and her mother, Hannah, a brisk, outgoing woman who worked for many years as a lab technician. Hannah adored her only child and devoted herself to helping Danielle become the exceptional individual Hannah knew she could be. Unfortunately, she went a bit overboard. Quite a bit, according to Danielle. As far back as Danielle could remember, Hannah hovered over her, instructing, encouraging, criticizing, and pushing her to "live up to her potential." Hoping to obtain her mother's acceptance and approval as all children do, Danielle did her best to comply with Hannah's wishes, but Danielle's best efforts always seemed to fall short of her mother's expectations.

"How could you impress a woman who made perfectly symmetrical patterns in the carpet when she vacuumed and color-coordinated her clothing in her closet?" Danielle commented. "No matter what I did, it wasn't good enough. If I came home with a B, my mother told me that I could and should have gotten an A." And if Danielle got an A? "She'd ask about my other classes," Danielle replied. "She'd say, 'We can't have you slacking off in any of them, now can we?' "

Hannah kept her love and acceptance just beyond Danielle's grasp. She made it clear that she expected a great deal from her daughter, and then when Danielle did what was expected, Hannah raised her expectations. "No time to rest on our laurels," she would say. "There's always room for improvement somewhere."

Although Hannah was only trying to live up to her own high standards for being a good mother and only doing what she sincerely believed was in her daughter's best interest, her approach ensured that Danielle was always "a day late and a dollar short." Well intentioned or not, Hannah's overbearing, hypercritical, and intimidating behavior left her daughter feeling inadequate and unloved. Danielle's sense of "not measuring up" and her belief that "no matter how hard I try, I'll always fail or be disappointed" would haunt her for years to come.

As an adult, Danielle no longer needed her mother to set perfectionist, unrealistic goals for her. She had become her own relentless taskmaster. When she made a mistake or fell short of her goals, she no longer needed her mother to remind her of what she could or should have done, she automatically blamed herself for anything that went wrong, administering large doses of self-punishment that left her feeling all the more inadequate and anxious about possibly making mistakes in the future. Finally, Danielle no longer needed her mother to rob her of her sense of pride and accomplishment. Nothing was good enough to receive her own approval. Danielle had internalized the messages that made her miserable as a child, replaying them in her own mind and thus making herself miserable as an adult.

In a sense your parents as well as other people who had an impact on you become a part of you, and the messages they conveyed to you through their words and actions still guide you through your life today. If the messages you received validated your self-worth, supported your efforts to be yourself, encouraged you to take on new challenges, or let you know that you were okay even when your behavior was not, then your "old tapes" or "inner voices" supply comfort and words that prod you in positive new directions as well as enable you to cope effectively with life's crises. The exact opposite occurs when you listen to inner voices that reiterate the messages of a perfectionist parent like Hannah, an uninterested one like Joel's father, or an overprotective one who constantly warned you not to attempt new endeavors because you were bound to be disappointed or get hurt. The "guidance," and more often than not the self-punishment, provided by those old tapes can lead to depression.

When Danielle met Greg, something clicked right away; some instinct told her that she and this brash, exacting pediatric surgeon were "made for each other." Moments after they began conversing at a mutual friend's party, it became vitally important for Greg to like her, and Danielle did her best to impress him. On their first date Greg told Danielle about his previous marriage and his reasons for leaving it. As Danielle listened to Greg enumerate his ex-wife's flaws, she automatically began evaluating herself, wondering if she would "qualify" to become Greg's partner. Never pausing to ponder the harshness of Greg's marital postmortem, Danielle felt an enormous sense of relief each time Greg mentioned a fault that she did not have. She also heard herself claiming to love sailing as much as Greg did, even though she had never been on a sailboat. When Danielle got home after that date, she anxiously reviewed everything she had said or done. In fact, she stayed awake all night worrying that Greg had not liked her and would not call her again.

Although Danielle was not consciously aware of it, she had fallen back into her old familiar role as the approval-seeking child. Greg, in turn, took on the trappings of the powerful but hard-to-please parent, the role Hannah had once played and one for which he was perfectly cast. In many ways he was a carbon copy of Danielle's mother. He worked in a medical profession that suited a precise, logical, no-nonsense nature that was like Hannah's. Setting extraordinarily high standards for himself and everyone else, as Hannah did, Greg unwittingly "pushed the same buttons" that Danielle's mother had, and Danielle responded accordingly by feeling that she was not and never would be "good enough" to please Greg.

Without intending to, you, too, may get involved with people who convey the same messages you received as a child, who confirm what you already think about yourself and provide opportunities to reenact scenes that delighted or disturbed you the first time around. Subconsciously you try to make up for something you missed out on during childhood or to experience again what you had then and miss as an adult. You choose a lover or a spouse who is similar to your parents in subtle or not so subtle ways. At some intuitive, not quite conscious level you immediately "recognize" people you will be able to relate to in ways that are familiar and comfortable (although not necessarily beneficial) for you.

This can be a healthy occurrence even if your choices baffle friends and family. Regrettably, and as was certainly the case for Danielle, the process often goes awry. Instead of making up for childhood difficulties, you simply perpetuate them, and this can contribute to a chronic case of the blues.

LIFE EXPERIENCE FACTORS

Not every factor that contributes to DD dates all the way back to your childhood. You could have been blessed with an uneventful home life. Your parents' child-rearing practices, imperfect as they may have been, may have done little significant damage to your self-esteem. Yet you could still come down with a chronic case of the blues. Following are five life experiences that you can have as a teenager or as an adult that can set you on a downhill course to long-lasting, low-grade depression.

1. *Adjustment problems during adolescence.* Adolescence is a difficult developmental stage for us all. As you struggle to establish your own independent identity but with only the foggiest notion of who you want to be, it becomes vitally important to fit in with and be accepted by your peers. For one reason or another you may be unable to accomplish that task. As one DD sufferer, Judy, a travel agent in her early thirties, put it, "My high school was divided into cliques, and I didn't qualify for membership in any of them. I wasn't a cheerleader or a jock or a brain. I wasn't a hippie or a greaser. I wasn't even a nerd, just one of those wandering nobodies. I had transferred from another school district, so I didn't even have my grade school friends to pal around with. I spent four long, lonely years feeling like an outsider, wanting to but now knowing how to

get on the inside." This individual's feelings of alienation and despair are standard fare for teenagers and obviously do not lead to DD for everyone who has them. For some, however, and especially those being influenced by any of the factors already described, feeling "left out in the cold" during adolescence erodes an already fragile sense of self-worth and does enough damage to leave them prone to the blues.

2. *Troublesome life transitions.* When Andrea graduated from the Parsons School of Design, she had high hopes of a meteoric rise to fame and fortune in the fashion industry. What she got was a rude awakening.

"I practically papered New York with my résumés," she said. "I went to every design house with my portfolio, the garments I'd designed and the glowing letters of recommendation from my instructors at Parsons. I thought I'd just sit back, wait for the offers to come in, and pick the one that seemed most promising." Two months after graduation, Andrea had not received a single job offer that lived up to her expectations. Andrea's transition from "star student" to "just another entry-level job applicant" was disheartening to say the least. "It was a crushing blow," she declared. "I didn't want to move back home, so I got a waitressing job and spent most nights drowning my sorrow at parties and dance clubs. I couldn't face the fact that things weren't happening the way I wanted them to."

Eventually Andrea became so disillusioned that she decided to move to Los Angeles, where she could get a normal, not particularly taxing job and "maybe do a little designing" in her spare time. Because she was off-balance, downhearted, and not thinking clearly, she never considered that she did not know a soul in California, did not own a car in which to get around, and could not afford to buy one. She inadvertently backed herself into a corner and set herself up for a case of the blues that would last for the next five years.

Life transitions such as entering the work force or retiring from it, getting married, having children, relocating, and so on, bring with them new rules, new surroundings, new expectations, and new relationships. They may also force you to give up or revamp old ties to family and friends, old dreams, and old ways of conducting yourself. In other words, you have to change. Sometimes, like Andrea, you may be unwilling or ill-equipped to do that. You may feel overwhelmed, frustrated, or disillusioned and can become depressed, usually only for a brief period but in some cases for a long, long time.

3. *Losses and life crises.* As previously discussed, grief and sorrow are natural and appropriate feelings when someone you love dies, when you get divorced or a love affair ends, and when you experience financial setbacks or become a crime victim. Sometimes these losses and life crises land such a crushing blow that you never fully recover—and end up with DD. In other instances you almost seem to recover too quickly, as if the loss had not really affected you at all.

Bouncing back from a crisis in record time may not be as healthy as it looks. It often means that instead of working through your unsettling emotions, you buried them alive. When they come back to haunt you, as they invariably do, you may end up with a chronic case of the blues.

Connie is a prime example of this sort of delayed reaction. When Connie had her miscarriage, it hardly seemed to faze her. She was sad and tearful for a day or two. Ten years later she vaguely recalled having frightening thoughts about being unable to control anything that happened to her and one particularly morbid idea that kept gnawing at her: "I thought that because I was a good person I was protected from tragedies like that, but I was wrong. Life is full of grief and sadness. No matter what I do, horrible things will happen."

After several attempts to banish that thought from her mind, Connie succeeded and got on with her life as if there never had been a miscarriage. But as Connie would realize during a therapy session more than a decade later, that morbid idea never really went away. It remained in her subconscious, and like an invisible toxic gas, leaked out ever so slowly, dampening her spirits until she constantly felt blue.

4. *Chronic, unresolved, yet realistic life problems.* Although you may not respond by becoming depressed, certain circumstances, environments, or ongoing relationships can be depressing. Poverty, unemployment, ill health, painful or disabling medical problems, stormy interactions with parents, children, spouses, or friends—all of these are conditions that can, quite understandably, lead to a chronic case of the blues.

5. *Stress.* In addition to their potentially depressing effect, life transi-

tions, losses, or life crises and ongoing life problems produce stress, a generalized physical and emotional response to everyday or extraordinary demands.

Your cave-dwelling ancestors experienced stress when they encountered a threat to their physical survival, setting off an early warning system that prepared them to flee from a predator or to stand and fight. Although today's stressors are more often mental and emotional than physical, they trigger this same archaic "fight or flight" response, pumping adrenaline through your veins and putting various bodily systems on the alert.

This vigilant state lasted for only brief periods of time for your prehistoric ancestors: The flight or fight was made, the individual survived or was destroyed, and whatever the outcome, the stress ended. But modern-day sources of stress tend to be long-lasting, and you have a third option for survival: coping with stress by changing circumstances that are within your control and adapting to or accepting those that are not. Unfortunately, the symptoms of DD as well as other factors contributing to your depression can prevent you from effectively coping with everyday demands. Like most DD sufferers, you may be under more stress than people who do not have dysthymia, and your perpetual state of emergency preparedness can adversely affect your body chemistry.

SUSCEPTIBILITY PLUS

None of the factors I have described in this chapter actually *gives* you DD. They increase your susceptibility to it, but many people who are genetically vulnerable to mood disorders do not now and may never have DD. Although they get down in the dumps from time to time, they do not develop the attitudes, beliefs, and behavior patterns that sustain a chronic case of the blues. Their experiences, and more important, how they interpret their experiences, do not leave them with the blue mood mind-set you may have.

To understand what I mean by a blue mood mind-set, just think of Joel, who believed that adulthood was a joyless struggle and that life was so dangerous and unpredictable, the best he could do was ride out the storm. Or think of Danielle, who saw herself as inadequate, unlovable, and powerless, and who was convinced that if she tried to succeed or be happy, she would inevitably fail or be disappointed. Connie provides another example. Her mind-set was almost entirely subconscious, yet her belief that life was full of grief and sadness—and no matter what she did, horrible things would happen—permeated every moment of every day.

What Is in Your Mind-Set? Open your notebook to a clean page and fill the page with the conclusions you came to as a result of both your childhood experiences and more recent events. Do this by completing the following sentences:

> I am . . .
> Most people . . .
> The world is . . .
> When I think about my future, I see . . .

Do not stop after completing each sentence once. Use the stems as many times as you like and keep writing until you run out of conclusions.

By completing this exercise you may have identified what the therapist and author Dr. Aaron Beck calls the "cognitive triad" of depression. The triad includes your perceptions of yourself, the world (including the people in it), and your future. These "cognitions," or ideas, influence nearly everything you think, feel, and do in the present. People who are depressed have the following three cognitions: They see themselves as worthless, inadequate, inherently flawed, deprived, powerless, and unlovable; see the world as dangerous, hostile, unpredictable, and full of opportunities to fail or be hurt (the people in it are perceived as critical, demanding, uncaring, untrustworthy, and punishing); see the future as holding more of the same—more hardship, more suffering, more disappointment, and more failure.

If your finished sentences resemble these perceptions, then you may have a blue mood mind-set. On a day-to-day, moment-to-moment basis, you probably are not aware of your blue point of view and how it influences you. Your negative, blues-generating attitudes and beliefs are so much a part of you and so automatic that they slip by unnoticed, doing their dirty work. But noticed or not, your blue mood mind-set keeps you down in the dumps. To see how, consider the following example.

Let us say there is a situation in which two people have a minor car accident. They are mutually at fault, and after exchanging telephone numbers and insurance information, they go their separate ways. One driver's attitude is: "I'm basically a good person and a careful driver, but accidents happen to everyone now and then. I'm glad this one wasn't serious and that nobody got hurt." She resumes her day without further ado. While the accident certainly is not the highlight of her afternoon, she puts the misfortune into perspective and goes about her business without much difficulty.

The other driver, however, cannot leave the incident behind. His attitude is: "I'm such a jerk. I should have known something like this would happen. After all, I draw trouble like a magnet." He berates himself, blames himself for the entire episode, and is soon recalling every mishap he has ever had behind the wheel. If he does not conclude that his hopelessly inadequate driving is at fault, then he will decide that his "rotten luck" must be. He's "destined" to be hit by every lousy driver on the road, he thinks. As the afternoon wears on, he continues to brood and cannot give his full attention to his work. Things begin to go wrong. He makes an accounting error, arrives late for a meeting because he had stopped in the men's room and ended up "lost in thought" by the paper towel dispenser. The accident has "ruined" his day, and he is in no mood for the evening of socializing he had scheduled. He cancels his plans, orders a pizza, and "zonks out" in front of the television.

The first driver went on with her day, but thanks to his depressive mind-set, the second driver got stuck in a blue mood.

THE WAY OUT: LOOKING AT YOU NOW

Almost every contributing factor dates back to your recent or distant past. You were not responsible for what happened to you then, and you cannot travel back through time to change it. But you *are* responsible for your thoughts, feelings, and actions today, and you can change *them*. You did not plant the seeds that grew into a self-defeating blue mood mind-set. However, over the years you have watered and fertilized that crop of unproductive attitudes and beliefs. You can stop now. You *can* weed out the ideas that are working against you and plant new, more productive and realistic ideas in their place. Indeed, to overcome the blues, you must. The good news is that unlike the factors that may have started your downward spiral, you *can* change the aspects of your life-style that are perpetuating it.

The way out of DD can be found by looking at what you are doing now and recognizing how your thoughts, feelings, behaviors, and relationships today virtually guarantee that your blues won't go away. That is called riding the blue mood merry-go-round. The next chapter explains how you do it and where to find the switch that will stop the ride so you can get off.

4

Riding the
Blue Mood
Merry-Go-Round

Judy, the travel agent who is in her early thirties, had been blue for the past two and a half years. Her family history of depression and her own academic difficulties during high school and college may have left Judy susceptible to DD. She still described herself as "not too bright, sort of slow on the uptake," and believed that she had to "work twice as hard to do half as well" as other people. With the possible exception of being single and wishing she was not, however, there was little that could be called distressing in Judy's life today.

Nonetheless, her black moods followed her. They seemed to come from nowhere as she tried to do things that would make her feel better. Recently, for example, having accepted an invitation to a co-worker's birthday party and having purchased a new outfit for the occasion, Judy was, as she put it, "ready and willing to enjoy myself. I looked good. I felt good. I even met an interesting, good-looking single guy." But somewhere along the line—and Judy could not say when or why—her mood took a nosedive. "By midnight, I was home stuffing myself with a whole Sara Lee cheesecake and fighting back tears," she admitted.

Beverly, a forty-one-year-old bank teller and divorced mother of two, reported a similar experience. "It was one of those Monday holidays when the bank was closed but the schools weren't," Beverly explained. "I got some chores done in the morning and felt good about that. In fact, I was feeling so much better than usual that I decided to treat myself to shopping and lunch before the kids got home."

The shopping went without a hitch. "I even found the perfect shoes to go with a dress I planned to wear to the bank manager's retirement dinner," Beverly recalled. Still in good spirits, she decided to try a new restaurant that her co-workers had given rave reviews. She was "famished," another plus. Unlike Judy, Beverly tended to undereat when she was blue.

"Nothing out of the ordinary happened," Beverly commented, listing a number of things that could have gone wrong. "I didn't get caught in traffic or have trouble parking. In fact, I found a space right away. There wasn't a line to wait in at the restaurant. Everything was going remarkably well."

But less than fifteen minutes later, Beverly's blues—which had been her almost constant companion for the past four years—were back. By the time the waitress brought her meal, Beverly was too miserable to eat it. In what seemed like a split second and for no apparent reason, she had lost her appetite, her energy, her "good" feelings, and any glimmer of hope that her depressed condition was improving.

"That always happens to me," Beverly claimed. "I start getting back to normal, start feeling okay, but then in a flash I'm down again. It's like some mysterious force dropped a net of depression on top of me.

One minute it's not there, and the next I'm hopelessly tangled up in it."

Ralph, a twenty-seven-year-old lawyer, was even more fatalistic about his chronic case of the blues. His moods were "just there" when he woke up in the morning and intensified as the day wore on. "Like a cold," he said. "You start out with the sniffles and by nightfall you have a fever, sore throat, and a headache too. You don't have any control over that. That just happens." And according to Ralph, so did his blue moods.

SWITCHES THAT ACTIVATE THE MERRY-GO-ROUND

Like Connie, Joel, Danielle, and other DD sufferers I've introduced thus far, Judy, Beverly, and Ralph are trapped on the blue mood merry-go-round and you may be too. You may not remember buying a ticket, and you certainly are not enjoying the ride. Your blues have seeped into all areas of your life, adversely affecting the way you feel about yourself and your circumstances, how you interpret the events that occur around you, your interactions with other people, and virtually everything you do or do not do on a given day or over an extended period of time. You are probably well aware of this ripple effect.

However, like Judy, Beverly, and Ralph, you may not recognize the countereffect—the way your thoughts, behavior patterns, interactions, and so on, perpetuate your blue mood in general as well as trigger or intensify the blues in specific situations. Although you may be inclined to believe that fate, rotten luck, or some other external force is preventing your blues from going away, if you look closely, you will be able to see your own contribution—the ways in which you unwittingly set the blue mood merry-go-round in motion and keep it moving. You will also find the switches you can flip to stop the ride.

ON A RUNAWAY TRAIN OF EMOTION

If I were to ask those of you who have a chronic case of the blues why you picked up this book and what you hope to get from it, chances are that you would reply, "I want to *feel* better" or "I don't want to *feel* this way anymore." Because seemingly endless feelings of sadness, despondency, hopelessness, and helplessness can be the most disturbing symptoms of DD, the affective or emotional component of a blue mood is often the first one that comes to mind and the one you most want to remedy. So let's start there and take a closer look at Judy's experiences before, during, and after her co-worker's birthday party. As you will see, every move Judy made—from buying a new outfit to eating a whole cheese-cake at midnight—was dictated by her emotions.

Judy recalled that "when Wendy invited me to the party, I felt really flattered. It was such a nice gesture on her part, so I said yes right away." But then it dawned on Judy that since she did not know Wendy very well, she probably would not know most of the guests at the party. She began worrying about having nothing of interest to say to anyone and that she would spend the entire evening "standing alone in a corner like some stupid wallflower." Hoping that looking terrific would compensate for her intellectual and conversational deficits, Judy spent all day Saturday frantically shopping for a "perfect" outfit.

Exhausted by her quest, Judy tried to take a nap before the party. "Only I couldn't sleep," she recalled. "Each time I began to drift off, my heart started thumping like crazy, and I'd be wide awake again."

Feeling upset because her hair had "frizzed" and a bit lightheaded because she had been too nervous to eat lunch or dinner, Judy sat in her car for quite some time before she mustered up enough courage to join the merrymaking in Wendy's backyard. When she did, she recognized that she might have "done all that worrying for nothing." Three people Judy did know immediately came up to her and told her she looked sensational. Then a "fantastic-looking guy" offered to get her a drink, and in no time at all they were engaged in a spirited conversation about the Chicago Cubs. Judy liked baseball and, thinking that it might make her more interesting to men, she had gone out of her way to learn as much as she could about the game. Her plan was paying off. "Pete seemed really impressed," Judy acknowledged, but still she noticed herself waiting for him to lose interest, to "move on to someone more attractive, more intelligent." He did not.

"The longer he stayed and talked, the more uncomfortable I felt," Judy said. "My pulse was racing, and I was having a hard time catching my breath. I went right off the deep end when he said he had tickets to a Cubs game and asked me if I'd like to go. I don't know exactly what came over me, but there I was telling him that I was busy when I knew I wasn't and muttering something about maybe doing it some other time." Then Judy "bolted" for the bathroom. Feeling embarrassed, angry at herself, and "like a real idiot," Judy avoided Pete for the rest of the evening. "I was just too humiliated to face him," she explained. "And every time I noticed him looking over at me, I felt awful, like I'd blown this great opportunity to be with a great guy, like I'd lost yet another chance to be happy."

Considering this sequence of events and emotions, it was no wonder that Judy ended up in her kitchen binge-eating and feeling lonely, disgusted, and depressed. But Judy did not see that connection. Because her attention was focused only on the end result—another late night bout of the blues—she did not give a second thought to the circumstances that produced those results and sincerely believed that her depression had come out of nowhere. Only after she consciously reconstructed her experiences did Judy realize that a "runaway train of emotion" had carried her full speed ahead into that blue mood.

Although Judy noticed that her mood had taken a nosedive after she experienced emotions typically associated with the blues (loneliness, self-loathing, loss, sadness, and so on), the anxiety and obsessive worrying about her own inadequacies that began earlier in the day were the feelings that actually served as Judy's emotional entry point to a depressed mood. Any unsettling emotion (guilt, anger, frustration, confusion, doubt, disappointment) can have the same effect, and it is not at all uncommon to feel several emotions during a single event. Your *reaction* to those feelings flips the switch that sets the blue mood merry-go-round in motion. I emphasized the word "reaction" because your response to your emotions and not the emotions themselves are what get you into trouble.

Emotional Glitches. Feelings are natural, useful parts of yourself that let you know when something going on within or around you requires your attention. As you well know, not all feelings are unpleasant, but even when they are, they can be the stimulus for positive actions. Feeling angry when the sound of heavy metal music is rattling your walls (and your nerves) can motivate you to go next door and ask your neighbor to turn down his stereo. Thus, you get something you want or need (in this case, peace and quiet) because of an emotion that initially caused you distress or discomfort. Similarly, feeling anxious about a speech you have to deliver can prompt you to prepare it with care or rehearse it in front of a friend, enabling you to effectively avert the disaster you were anticipating. In addition, your emotions can be the gateway to greater self-awareness, self-understanding, and personal growth, allowing you to put past experiences into perspective, move through the grieving process, let go of old resentments, or discover new ways for coping with difficult situations.

Unfortunately, if you are a DD sufferer, you will rarely see such positive potential or educational value in your unsettling emotions. Instead, you may look upon painful, unpleasant, or even slightly uncomfortable feelings as enemies to be fought and conquered. Or you may view them as overpowering forces that you cannot begin to control. You feel victimized by them. Instead of feeling and expressing your emotions or taking action to resolve whatever might be at the heart of them, you fall into one of the following traps:

- You may go out of your way to avoid situations that stir up certain emotions, most notably anxiety. In an effort to keep unpleasant feelings at bay, you stay away from socializing, speaking up at staff meetings, going shopping by yourself, taking college courses, getting medical checkups, or other activities. In the process you limit your opportunities to experience pleasure, closeness, or a sense of accomplishment and pride. Indeed, you may be left with feelings that are equally or more distressing than the ones you were trying to avoid—namely, loneliness, lethargy, hopelessness, and depression. Furthermore, you do not learn that situations may not be as bad as you think they are, that mistakes are not fatal, that problems can be solved, and that you are not as powerless as your blue mood has led you to believe.
- You may try to bury or anesthetize your painful feelings, pushing them to the back of your mind, numbing them with alcohol or drugs, or stuffing them down deep inside of you by stuffing yourself with food. The "anesthetic" you choose can create additional problems for you. The enormous amount of energy it takes to not feel the way you feel can leave you drained and exhausted. But perhaps worst of all, in the process of deadening unpleasant emotions you deaden positive ones as well. When you flush one feeling, you end up flushing them all. Instead of feeling better, you feel numb and disconnected, or as Joel put it, you "sleepwalk through life like a zombie."
- You may go to the opposite extreme and become preoccupied,

even obsessed, with your "bad," depressed feelings. Hardly a moment passes when you do not notice them. You examine and reexamine them, berating yourself for feeling the way you do and getting angry at yourself for not "snapping out of" your depression. If your mood should lift, you experience no sense of relief. Positive stimuli cannot get through to you because you are too busy looking for signs that your blue mood is about to return. Like a child poking at and tearing the scab off a wound, you prevent yourself from healing.

- You may do absolutely nothing. Viewing your feelings as a hostile and uncontrollable force that spontaneously attacks you, you sit around waiting for your feelings to disappear just as spontaneously.
- You may assume that feelings are facts and act accordingly, which is precisely what Judy did when she rejected Pete's invitation to go to a Cubs game. She was *afraid* that Pete would discover she was boring (which was how she saw herself) and reject her. Automatically, and in all probability unconsciously, assuming that being afraid meant that there really was something to fear, she immediately took action to avert the disaster, to prevent Pete from doing what she feared he would do but which, *in reality*, he might not have done. Judy was correct when she said she had "lost out on yet another chance to be happy." That is all too often the outcome of assuming that how you feel about a situation is what is actually happening in that situation.
- Similarly and perhaps even more commonly, you may assume that you are the way you feel. Thus, *feeling* stupid about a mistake you made convinces you that you are a stupid person. Feeling foolish is taken to mean that you are a fool, and feeling that you have failed in a specific situation reinforces the notion that you are a hopeless failure in general. Needless to say, this does nothing for your already ailing sense of self-worth or your already self-defeating image of yourself as powerless to overcome your chronic case of the blues.

These *responses* to feelings that are integral parts of daily living are the emotional "glitches" that get you stuck on the blue mood merry-go-round, and they are correctable. Little can be or needs to be done to the feelings themselves. There is nothing actually wrong with them. Adjustments in the behavior you engage in because of your feelings *is* required, however, and plenty of tinkering may need to be done on the line of thinking that triggers or intensifies unsettling emotions.

THINKING YOURSELF INTO A BLUE MOOD

Staring gloomily at the food on her plate, Beverly thought: *"I'm such a loser. My life is such a mess. How can I help but be depressed when nothing, not even a simple shopping trip and lunch, turns out the way I want it to?"*

Beverly was right about one thing: The restaurant meal was not turning out to be the "treat" she had originally intended it to be. Sideswiped by the sudden, seemingly unexplainable return of her blue mood, she was most unlikely to enjoy her walnut chicken salad, and she had already forgotten how much she had enjoyed her shopping trip or how productive she had felt when she completed her household chores earlier that day. Where had those good feelings gone?

To answer that question, let's back up a bit to the moment when the restaurant's young hostess greeted Beverly at the door and asked, "Are you eating alone?" The question sounded like a derogatory comment to Beverly. "I couldn't help thinking that she saw me as some kind of loser," Beverly recalled, "that she was asking herself, 'What's the matter with this woman? Doesn't she have any friends to eat lunch with her?' " When Beverly looked around the room and saw that all of the other customers were in pairs or groups, she began wondering about that herself.

When the hostess led her to a table in the center of the room, Beverly thought: *"I'm going to stick out like a sore thumb sitting here. Everyone in the room can see that I'm alone."* Beverly could have asked to be seated elsewhere, but she did not. *"The hostess would think I was a troublemaker,"* Beverly predicted, *"and I'd just draw more attention to myself by causing a scene."* Ironically, she changed her tune once the hostess walked away. *"I should have asked for a different table,"* Beverly berated herself and thought of at least a dozen assertive friends who would have done that. She was soon comparing herself to them and criticizing herself for not being more like them. *"Let's face it,"* she thought. *"You're a doormat. You won't speak up for yourself. You can't do anything right."* Once again down in the dumps, Beverly concluded, *"Things were going so well, but now my whole day is ruined."* And when a perverse inner voice added, *"As usual,"* it took only a short mental hop for Beverly to label herself a loser, judge her entire life to be a mess, and decide that it always would be.

As you can see, the path from the restaurant entrance (where Beverly felt "normal" and even somewhat hopeful) to the table (where she felt miserable and hopeless) was littered with assumptions, negative predictions, self-reproaching "shoulds," unfavorable comparisons to other people, and overgeneralizations. Clearly, a "mysterious force" had not "dropped a net of depression" on Beverly. She had ensnared herself. It was Beverly's own *unproductive thinking* that had instigated the return of her blue mood.

COGNITIVE GLITCHES

The concept that people can and often do think themselves into a depressed emotional state is the backbone of cognitive therapy, an approach that was developed by Dr. Aaron Beck and popularized in the book *Feeling Good*, by Dr. David Burns. According to Beck, Burns, and other cognitive therapists, your thinking has become dysfunctional or unproductive and is apt to lead to a depressed mood when it:

- makes it more difficult for you to cope with life experiences, including ordinary, everyday ones like dining alone in a restaurant;
- creates unnecessary confusion, stirring up anxiety or a "hornet's nest" of other emotions;
- causes needless discomfort and inappropriate or extreme reactions, intensifying emotional pain or increasing the stress of already stressful situations;
- leads to self-defeating behavior or prevents you from achieving your goals;
- prompts you (DD sufferers in particular) to draw the conclusion that "the way things are" is carved in granite, and you are utterly powerless to change them.

Many of Beverly's thoughts fit this description. So did some of Judy's. She stirred up an internal "hornet's nest" as soon as it dawned on her that there would be people she did not know at her co-worker's birthday party. She caused herself "needless discomfort" by conjuring up images of spending the evening "standing alone in a corner like some stupid wallflower." In addition, believing that she was "just lucky to run into a guy who liked baseball" and predicting that "once he really got to know me he'd find out that I'm boring and not too bright," most definitely had a hand in Judy's self-defeating acts of turning down Pete's invitation and avoiding him for the rest of the evening.

Of course, neither Beverly nor Judy set out to think herself into a blue mood. Indeed, they were not fully aware of doing it. Many of their thoughts were hidden from them and called the shots from the recesses of their minds without ever surfacing into consciousness.

This happens to all of us countless times each day. Take an "automatic" task such as brushing and flossing your teeth. Behind this routine is a whole line of thinking that includes everything you ever learned about how to brush and floss as well as the reasons for doing it: *"Cavities are uncomfortable and expensive to get filled. Proper dental care helps prevent cavities. If I brush and floss, I stand a better chance of warding off cavities."* And so on.

Naturally, you do not "hear yourself" go through this chain of thought every time an opportunity to brush presents itself, but those thoughts are there nonetheless, firmly planted in your subconscious. Based on them, you make choices (to brush or not to brush) and act accordingly.

Hidden thoughts that trigger emotional reactions operate in much the same way. When hidden thoughts are also unproductive, they influence you even though you are unaware of their influence and, like Judy and Beverly, you end up in a blue mood without comprehending how you got there. Fortunately, if you try, you can uncover your hidden thoughts by tracing the path you took from point A (a stressful or upsetting situation) to point C (an unsettling or painful emotional state). Strategies that appear later in this book will show you how to do that, enabling you to begin correcting the cognitive glitches in your mood.

Of course, not all unproductive thoughts are hidden. Some—such as Beverly's assumption that the hostess thought she was a loser—are fleeting. They emerge in your conscious mind for an instant, then disappear. Once such thoughts are gone, you forget that you ever had them. Other thoughts—such as Beverly's sense that she stuck out like a sore thumb—come and go. Rather than being forgotten, they are temporarily replaced by other thoughts. If someone asked you what you were thinking, you could easily recall the thought and then answer the question.

Many thoughts are habitual. They automatically come to mind whenever a particular stimulus is present. For instance, whenever Danielle picks up the phone and hears her mother's voice, she invariably thinks,

"What have I done now?," tenses up, and braces herself for a lecture that may or may not be forthcoming. Similarly, whenever Judy notices that someone with whom she is talking seems the least bit distracted, she immediately concludes that she is boring that person. Finally, if you have ever gotten the idea that you left your door unlocked or a cigarette burning and could not get the idea out of your head until you checked the door or the ashtray, you know there are thoughts that linger in your mind no matter how hard you try not to think about them. Since all of these thoughts are out in the open, the problem with them is not that you do not recognize them but, rather, that you believe they are *accurate* and act accordingly.

Thoughts do *not* replicate reality. Indeed, the gap between what you think or believe to be true and what you know or can prove to be an irrefutable fact can be as wide as the Grand Canyon. If Beverly had realized this, she could have caught her first unproductive thought and countered it by saying to herself, "Hey, wait a minute. I don't actually know what the hostess is thinking. She probably seats plenty of parties of one every day and thinks nothing of it. Besides, it was my decision to eat lunch alone, and there is nothing wrong with that." In other words, Beverly could have replaced her inaccurate, unproductive thought with a more productive and in all probability more accurate one, thus cutting her blue mood off at the pass. This is another blues-busting tactic that you will find later in this book.

In addition to stirring up feelings that lead you straight downhill into the blues, you can get yourself into trouble by making decisions based on your inaccurate ideas. For instance, although Beverly would have been more comfortable sitting at a different table, her thoughts (*"The hostess will think I'm a troublemaker. I'll call even more attention to myself if I cause a scene."*) prevented her from acting in her own best interest. Thanks to a decision based on "mind reading" and a negative prediction, she sat in the center of the room, feeling uncomfortable and self-conscious throughout her meal.

Similarly, Ralph, the lawyer mentioned earlier, had an unproductive way of assuming that his flaws were as obvious to everyone else as they were to him and that other people felt as sorry for him as he felt for himself. Consequently, whenever one of his colleagues or housemates asked him to come along to a concert or sporting event, he thought, *"He doesn't really want me to go. He only asked out of pity,"* and turned him down. Because of his distorted point of view, he did not do things that might have improved his depressed emotional state—which is the third way to set the blue mood merry-go-round in motion.

THE TASKS INCREASE THE BURDEN

As the sun streams through her window on a Saturday morning, Andrea composes a mental checklist of all the things she wants to get done that day. Each item—from varnishing the bookshelf that has been standing empty on sheets of newspaper for the past three months to looking for secondhand curtains at a flea market—sends her off on a tangent of one kind or another. Thinking about getting the car washed leads to thinking about what a "clunker" the car is, which leads to thoughts of the rude, sexist mechanic who services it and how much money she spends on repairs and how little money she has managed to save during the past five years she has lived in Los Angeles. Wearing herself out without moving a muscle, Andrea goes back to sleep.

Waking again at noon, she wanders into the kitchen, takes a relatively clean bowl and spoon out of the sink, and brings it, a carton of milk, and a box of sugar-coated cereal into the living room with her. She wishes she had a newspaper to read, but she still has not gotten around to calling about having one delivered. Andrea turns on the TV, but an hour later she could not tell you what she has seen. Lost in thought, she has not paid attention to what she was eating, either, and has finished the whole box of cereal without tasting any of it.

The remainder of Andrea's day continues in this random, hit-or-miss, semiconscious manner. By the end of it, she has reviewed everything that was wrong with her life ten times over but has not completed a single task on her mental to-do list.

Andrea's behavior is a symptom of her chronic case of the blues. It is also a surefire way to sustain her blue moods. Everywhere Andrea looks she sees half-finished projects, evidence of good, even brilliant ideas that have fallen by the wayside, signs that she is stuck in a rut from which she has little hope of extracting herself. Each night when she lists the tasks that she never "got around to," Andrea feels like a failure. And each morning, when she makes another, even longer list of tasks to accomplish, it seems painfully obvious that she will never be able to dig herself out of the deep, dark hole in which she finds herself.

Yet, if Andrea did just one or two things that she needed or wanted to do, she would not be quite as disgusted with herself. She would not spend quite as much time stewing and might make enough progress to see the light of day from a hole that is no longer quite as dark or deep.

BEHAVIORAL GLITCHES

As was apparent in Andrea's case, your action or inaction has consequences, and those consequences can sustain your blue mood.

- *Inactivity* leaves you with far too much time for wallowing in self-pity and ruminating about everything that is wrong with your life.
- *Lack of productivity* robs you of the sense of pride and accomplishment that comes along with a job well done. It leaves you with far too many reminders of your failure to follow through, your lack of stick-to-itiveness and other supposed character flaws, damaging your self-esteem.
- *Procrastination* leads to guilt and feelings of inadequacy and ineffectiveness.
- *Disorganization* makes your life seem all the more unmanageable, fueling your feelings of powerlessness, stirring up anxiety, and exacerbating DD symptoms of indecisiveness and poor concentration.
- *Self-destructive behaviors* such as drinking, overeating, compulsive spending, throwing temper tantrums, and so on, create new problems. If you find that, try as you might, you cannot discontinue those behaviors, your guilt, shame, self-loathing, and hopelessness are magnified tenfold.
- *Too many shoulds and not enough want-to's* prevent you from experiencing joy or pleasure. You simply do not *do* anything that feels good or gives you pleasure.

These are just a few of the behavior patterns that you, like millions of other DD sufferers, may have developed.

Just as many self-defeating thoughts are hidden, many self-defeating behaviors are habitual—deeply ingrained, automatic ways of operating on a daily basis and even more so in stressful situations. Joel, who tended to do nothing about meeting new people until his loneliness became intolerable, had picked up this habit from his father, who did nothing until his wife's major depressive episode reached crisis proportions. Joel had learned his behavior pattern during childhood, and you may have too. Or like Andrea, whose tendency not to get around to things was a recent development, you may not have fallen into your habit until *after* you came down with the blues. But no matter when or why you picked them up, you undoubtedly and perhaps unwittingly practiced your self-defeating behavior patterns until they became second nature to you. As a result you do not stop to consider your options, weigh the possible consequences, and make a choice about what you will do. You just do it. And each time you engage in that same depressing behavior pattern, you send current down the wire to the generator that runs the blue mood merry-go-round, guaranteeing that your blues will not go away. You can get different results, of course, by doing things differently.

SOMETIMES IT TAKES TWO TO BE BLUE

Several months before I met Danielle, she was commissioned to do a painting that would hang in the lobby of a very exclusive Manhattan high-rise building. "It was a real coup," she explained. "And I was pretty excited about it." She wanted Greg to be excited too and remembered thinking: *"This should really impress him. He'll be pleased by this."*

Danielle considered calling Greg to give him the news right away, but knowing that he might be too busy to talk to her, she decided to wait until they met for dinner. That left her the entire day to fantasize about how thrilled Greg would be and to imagine the wonderfully approving and encouraging words he would say. Unfortunately, Danielle's fantasies were as close as she would come to getting what she wanted.

You see, Greg had some good news of his own and, being the aggressive, "cut straight to the chase" type person that he was, he delivered that news immediately. As soon as he joined Danielle at their table, he announced that he had been asked to present a paper at a medical conference, a *very important* medical conference. For the next fifteen minutes he filled in the details.

By doing this, Greg "ruined" Danielle's surprise and tarnished her fantasy. A rapid downward spiral began. Listening to Greg go on about *his* "coup," Danielle wondered if her commission was all that impressive. *"I paint all the time,"* she thought. *"But what Greg was asked to do is really something special."* Her chances of getting the response she wanted from Greg seemed slim. *"He's not going to care about my news,"* she predicted. *"He's not going to be proud of me or tell me how pleased he is."* Feeling disappointed, Danielle showed little enthusiasm over Greg's triumph, and her end of the conversation consisted of a few flatly delivered expressions of "really" and "that's nice." *"If he cares about me, he'll notice that I'm upset"* was the hidden assumption behind Danielle's behavior.

Obviously not noticing, Greg plowed right on, saying, "I haven't even gotten to the best part." The conference was in Hawaii, and Danielle could come with him, he explained. In fact, he had already called his travel agent to make the arrangements.

"He didn't even stop to think that I might have work to do or a show scheduled," Danielle thought, silently fuming. *"That's how insignificant I am to him. If he loved me at all, he would have consulted me first."* Although righteous indignation and plain old anger were churning inside her, Danielle said nothing about it.

Well on her way to another bout of the blues, when Greg finally got around to asking about her day, Danielle claimed that "nothing much" had happened and blandly related the bare facts about her commission. "That's terrific," Greg said and requested more information. But Danielle just shrugged, and said, "There's not much to tell. It's just another painting."

Danielle wanted something from Greg but did not get it. She felt hurt, disappointed, and unloved; she "fell for" a series of unproductive thoughts and inaccurate assumptions and then behaved in a manner that guaranteed her need for Greg's approval, encouragement, and admiration would not be fulfilled (which also guaranteed that she would feel even more hurt, disappointed, and unloved). She was back on the blue mood merry-go-round, and her *interaction* with another person flipped the switch.

INTERPERSONAL GLITCHES

Depression is accompanied by many interpersonal problems that tend to prolong and complicate the depression. These problems are treated in Interpersonal Therapy, an approach to treating mood disorders that was developed by Drs. Gerald Klerman and Myrna Weissman after more than two decades of research with depressed patients at Yale, Harvard,

Columbia, and Cornell. Interpersonal Therapy is useful for DD sufferers who are apt to be socially isolated or to derive little satisfaction from the relationships they do have.

If you have a chronic case of the blues, chances are that you rarely get the feedback you need to confirm that you are attractive, lovable, competent, valued, or even acknowledged as a human being with needs and wishes that are worthy of attention and fulfillment. Instead—and as was certainly true for Danielle—your relationships and interactions tend to reinforce your low opinion of yourself and your conviction that you are powerless to get what you need or want out of life. Why? Because of one or more of the following interpersonal glitches.

- Symptoms of the blues—exhaustion, lethargy, constantly running to catch up on the things you should do, not wanting to bring other people down or just not feeling in the mood to socialize—can prompt you to withdraw from friends or family and avoid social situations. As your blues persist, so does your *isolating behavior,* leaving you with a limited number of social outlets, little or no emotional support, and few opportunities for pleasurable contact with other people.
- You may be so *anxious in social situations* and so preoccupied with your own anxious thoughts that you fail to receive or benefit from the positive signals that are being sent your way. This was certainly true for Judy, who derived no satisfaction whatsoever from the positive attention paid to her by Pete.
- You may *lack the social skills* you need to connect with and get to know new people as well as the *assertiveness skills* that could help you get what you want and need from interactions with people you already know.
- Already having an aversion to conflict, you may assume that there will be none in a good relationship. Consequently, whenever you and a friend, lover, or spouse argue or disagree, your entire relationship seems to be on the line, and you feel unhappy, even devastated. Or you may expect other people to know what you are feeling and act accordingly—as Danielle did when she thought that Greg would notice she was upset and do something to show that he cared. Because the people in your life are not mind readers, your expectation goes unmet, and you spend a great deal of your time feeling disappointed. A variation on this theme—believing that other people should have known that their words or actions would upset you—

means that you will spend a great deal of your time feeling angry and outraged. Frequently, a tendency to equate not doing something you want with not loving you causes trouble. *"If he loved me at all, he would have consulted me,"* Danielle thought, then concluded that Greg did not love her and continued her downward spiral into despair. These are just a few examples of the interpersonal glitch created by *unrealistic expectations for your relationships*.

- In your already depressed condition, you may need so much comfort and reassurance that you *"burn out" people who do care about you* and sincerely want to be there for you. For example, Marcia, a slightly overweight yet quite attractive kindergarten teacher, felt so worthless and unattractive that she had convinced herself "it was only a matter of time until I lose the one bright spot in my life"—her husband, Jack. She depended on Jack to supply her with a steady stream of compliments, to give her hope when she felt hopeless, to encourage her to accomplish things and put her back together when she fell apart. Driven by her fear of losing this lifeline, Marcia constantly fished for compliments, asked for reassurance, consulted Jack before making any decision, and accused him of flirting with other women (when it was obvious to any outside observer that Marcia had his undivided attention).

  As you might expect, all of this had begun to take its toll on Jack, who said, "I love Marcia, but she is driving me away with her constant demands. I'm nearing the end of my rope." Sensing this, Marcia became more depressed and more dependent, continuing on a course that could eventually net her what she most feared.

  Although it does not always play itself out the way it did for Marcia and Jack, your blue moods initially elicit sympathetic and supportive responses. The people in your life try to help you feel better. But when you do not get better or when you get worse, other people get fed up and may break their ties with you completely or keep their contact with you to a bare minimum. Naturally, this only reinforces your perception that no one *really* cares about you.

- Finally, and to put it bluntly, *you can be a "real drag" to be around*. While in a blue mood, you may be cranky, oversensitive, pouty, irritable, and just plain difficult to deal with. You snap at people, burst into tears at the drop of a hat, reject well-intentioned overtures, and radiate negativity, leaving everyone in your life bruised and wary. Reaping the rewards of your own behavior, you no longer have to withdraw from or avoid people. They avoid you.

You may be tempted to blame your interpersonal problems on other people (who do not care about or cannot understand you). Don't! You need to take responsibility for your own issues. You can learn new skills and new ways of relating to people and by doing so begin to chase away the blues.

The components of a blue mood—feelings, thoughts, actions, and interpersonal interactions—are so intricately interconnected that a glitch in one area generally creates a glitch in another area and so on down the line. Soon your mood is being short-circuited in dozens of ways dozens of times each day. However, you rarely notice this while it is happening and may not even recognize it after the fact. That must change. Paying attention to subtle changes in your emotional state and identifying the individual components of your mood that are most likely to malfunction is the key to stopping and eventually getting off the blue mood merry-go-round. How do you do that? By self-monitoring, a process you can learn by conducting the following research study on yourself.

CONDUCTING A RESEARCH STUDY ON YOURSELF

As you will see, the self-monitoring measures that I am about to rec-ommend take time. Four weeks' time, to be exact. I encourage you to take all of that time and complete all of the steps. Follow through to the end!

The following self-monitoring strategy will enable you to uncover rea-sons for your long-standing blue mood. Unlike the predisposing factors you learned about in the last chapter, these reasons direct you to the solutions you have been hoping to find. What is more, the process itself provides certain benefits. First, it gives you an opportunity to take the healthy, objective, mindful part of yourself and bring it to bear on your dysthymic, depressed side. You have been doing the exact opposite for quite some time now, so the change in focus will be refreshing, even uplifting. Second, by concentrating on specific parts of your condition instead of looking at it as a huge, unmanageable whole, you will feel less powerless. Although making the blues go away in one fell swoop is still beyond your capabilities, correcting small pieces of the problem is some-thing you *can* do, and you will see a ray of hope. Finally, you will be developing a new positive habit of paying attention to what is happening within and around you, and with it, the potential to recognize and do something about upsetting circumstances *before* they send you plummeting into the pits of depression.

With that in mind, get out your notebook and make four copies of the Weekly Self-Monitoring Chart (table 1).

Week One: Five times a day (as noted on the chart), rate your mood and your energy level/physical condition. Use the following 1–10 rating scales:

    MOOD 10 = elation, feeling on top of the world

           1 = the pits, utterly depressed, as down as you can get

    ENERGY 10 = bursting with energy, feeling in peak condition

           1 = completely exhausted, worn out or aching all over

If you give yourself the same rating five times a day every day, you are probably operating on the assumption that you feel about the same all of the time; you're not really paying attention. That won't help you.

Week Two: Continue your ratings *and* in the space provided list the emotions you are experiencing or experienced between ratings. Be specific. You already know that you feel "blah" or blue. What else are you feeling—anger, frustration, resentment, sadness, confusion, jealousy, hopelessness, fear, anxiety, annoyance, self-doubt, disappointment? Remember that you can have several feelings at the same time and that pleasant feelings count. List them too.

Week Three: Continue rating and listing feelings. Also jot down (in the appropriate columns) any encouraging experiences or stressful/upsetting events that occurred between ratings.

Week Four: Continue rating, listing feelings, and keeping track of your experiences. In addition, set aside time each day or evening to analyze one of the stressful or upsetting situations you noted on your chart. It can be something you encountered that day or something you jotted down during Week Three. Conduct your analysis by answering in writing the following questions that were developed by James P. McCullough of Virginia Commonwealth University as part of his Cognitive-Behavioral Analysis System of Psychotherapy (C-BASP) for treating DD:

1. *What happened?* Describe the event objectively, as if it were a movie you were watching. Provide details in sequence (what happened first, next, and so on).
2. *What did it mean to you?* For instance, to Judy, her experiences at the birthday party meant that she had "lost another chance to be

TABLE 1
WEEKLY SELF-MONITORING CHART

		MOOD (1–10)	ENERGY (1–10)	FEELINGS	UPLIFTING EVENTS	STRESSFUL OR UPSETTING EVENTS
DAY #___	Waking					
	Mid-morning					
	Mid-afternoon					
	Early evening					
	Bedtime					
DAY #___	Waking					
	Mid-morning					
	Mid-afternoon					
	Early evening					
	Bedtime					
DAY #___	Waking					
	Mid-morning					
	Mid-afternoon					
	Early evening					
	Bedtime					

happy." Beverly concluded that "nothing, not even a simple shopping trip and lunch, turns out the way I want it to." And Danielle thought her experience meant that "no matter what I do, I'll never impress Greg." Try to identify what you told yourself, expected, or feared *during* the experience as well. Phrases such as "I can't," "I'll never," "If only I had," or calling yourself a jerk, a fool, a dope, or some other derogatory name are clues for answering this question.

3. *What were you feeling?*

4. *What was your role in the situation?* In response to what was happening, what did you do, say, or signal nonverbally? What didn't you do or say that you could have? For example, when Greg turned the spotlight on himself, Danielle "got quiet" and responded unenthusiastically (hoping that he would notice she was upset and give her some of the spotlight). When she learned that Greg had made plans without consulting her, she "swallowed" her anger and did nothing. And when Greg finally expressed interest in what had happened to her that day, she played down her news, presenting it as if it was as unimportant as she already assumed Greg would view it.

5. *How did the situation turn out for you?* What was its actual outcome? And how did that compare to . . .

6. *What did you want to happen (the desired outcome)?*

Once you have answered those questions, go back through your analysis and underline the possible problem areas—any thoughts, feelings, actions, or interactions that might have contributed to the stressful or upsetting nature of the event or prevented you from obtaining the outcome you desired.

At the end of the Fourth Week: Review your charts and other writings. Identify the patterns that emerged by completing sentences beginning with: I learned that I . . . , I discovered that I . . . , I noticed that I . . . , and so on.

Based on those patterns, identify some areas where changes or adjustments might help you to feel better. You don't need irrefutable proof. A hunch is fine. And rather than phrasing things negatively (that is, "I have to stop jumping to stupid conclusions" or "I'd better stop acting like such a doormat"), try putting your goals in the following framework: "If I could _____ [weigh the evidence before I draw conclusions or be more assertive] _____, I might feel better." Then prioritize your goals, giving number-one priority to the self-help measure you would be most willing to try, number-two priority to the one you are next most willing to try, and so on until all of your goals have a numerical ranking.

STARTING SOMEWHERE

"If I could get organized, I might feel better," Andrea wrote. Joel's response was, "If I could meet new people in places other than bars or singles functions, I might feel better." Danielle thought learning to be more assertive might be the place to start, and both Judy and Beverly concluded that they wanted to learn how to change their unproductive thought patterns to more productive ones. Your top priority goal may be similar to or different from theirs. It does not matter. Your own individual needs, problems, and interests determine which avenue for overcoming the blues you turn onto first. What does matter is beginning to recognize how you "self-produce" your blue moods and that you can self-produce the solution for them.

I began this chapter by present DD sufferers' prevailing point of view: that the blues come out of the blue. Chances are that you shared that perspective as well as the fundamental belief that invariably accompanies it: Because I am depressed and my depression is brought on by forces beyond my control, I am not responsible for the mess I am in, and there is nothing I can do about it. James McCullough calls this the "predominant cognitive fiction" subscribed to by dysthymic individuals, and it is precisely what the term "fiction" implies—patently untrue.

You now know that a chronic case of the blues does not "just happen." On a day-to-day, moment-to-moment basis, you contribute to your own depression and sustain it with thoughts and actions. You may not have been aware of your contribution in the past, but now that you are aware of it you may be able to do something about it.

You can start anywhere. Concentrating on one component will produce improvements in other areas and have a positive effect on your overall mood. But you *must* start somewhere because if you do not, you will remain on the blue mood merry-go-round and continue to suffer from your chronic case of the blues.

5

Emotional Switches and the Law of Inertia

F ive years ago when Andrea's search for a "promising" position in fashion design did not materialize, she moved to Los Angeles, took a computer programming course, and went to work in an office. Not particularly stimulating but not stressful either, the job paid reasonably well and was intended to be temporary—a means for Andrea to support herself until she got her life and her "real" career back on track. In fact, Andrea still thought of it that way. "I don't intend to do office work for the rest of my life!" she protested. "This is just something I'm doing to pay the rent. I still want to get into some aspect of the fashion business."

Just when did Andrea propose to do that? "When my self-esteem is up to par," she said, going on to explain that her opinion of herself was very low because of the "chaotic emotional climate" in her childhood home. Separating for the first time when she was four, Andrea's parents reconciled and split up a dozen times before they finally divorced when Andrea was ten. "They were so caught up in their own drama that they never had time for us kids," she said, and according to Andrea, this led to a "deficit of parental approval" that haunted her throughout her life. "We were very affluent, but my dependency needs weren't met," she said. She then pointed out that "unconscious conflicts" were making her depressed and preventing her from "actualizing myself or living up to my human potential."

After listening to this steady stream of psychological jargon, I was not surprised to learn that Andrea had been in therapy both as an adolescent and for the past four and a half years. When she added in the cost of the many self-help paperbacks she had purchased (and sometimes even read), Andrea estimated that she had already spent close to ten thousand dollars on the worthy cause of feeling better.

But what did her discourse have to do with staying in her supposedly temporary job? "Fashion is a tough, ultra-competitive business," she said. "You need self-confidence. When you don't have it, it's hard to make a start, and it gets harder by the minute." It quickly became apparent that Andrea had put her entire life on hold until her long-awaited self-esteem arrived and her chronic case of the blues went away.

"I know I should have more interests, do more with my life," Andrea commented, "but the state I'm in makes it hard to get started. I just don't have the energy." As you may recall, Andrea also ran out of energy before she finished the projects she did start. She rarely ran out of rationalizations, however. Andrea had yet to unpack a dozen boxes of belongings stacked in her bedroom. "I want to get the place painted first," she explained, "and add a built-in wall unit. But I haven't saved up the money yet."

Andrea felt cheated because she did not have the wildly exciting social life that she had expected to find in Los Angeles. Yet when her friend Maxie won two tickets for a weekend cruise to nowhere and asked

Andrea to go on it with her, Andrea hemmed and hawed and finally decided not to do it. "I know I might have had a good time," Andrea said, "but I just wasn't up to it. I had put on a few pounds, and I couldn't imagine going anywhere until I lost them."

By now you may be ready to shake Andrea until her teeth rattle. Her friend Maxie certainly was. "I'm so tired of hearing about why she can't do this or hasn't done that or isn't ready to do something else that I could scream," Maxie declared. "Andrea says that she went into therapy to get insight. Well, she got her money's worth all right. She has tons and tons of insight, not that it's done her a bit of good. I just don't see the point of sitting around like a bump on a log and waiting to get 'actualized.' If Andrea doesn't like the way her life is going, she should get off her butt and *do* something about it!"

INERTIA AND FORMS OF RESISTANCE

I certainly am not opposed to gaining insights about your condition and what might be causing it. Insight alone does not change anything, however. Simply understanding your problems, the underlying reasons for them, and the many things you *could* do to get out of your rut is not enough to make your blues go away. And it never will be. To overcome DD you must translate insight into action. You must actually *do* something to change your outlook, your habits, or your circumstances.

As you can see, Andrea did not do that. In fact, just about the only thing she did with her insight was use it to come up with excuses *not* to take action. When presented with alternatives or opportunities to change, the first two words Andrea uttered were "Yeah, but . . ." and then she proceeded to explain why she could not pursue that option—no matter what it was. Since conjuring up "perfectly good reasons" not to change is something virtually all DD sufferers have in common, if you have a chronic case of the blues, you probably do it too.

Although dysthymics' rationalizing looks like a willful refusal to act on their own behalf, their resistance to change is not malicious or even intentional. They do not wake up in the morning and decide to be depressed, nor do they knowingly choose to stay on the same depressing course even though alternative routes are available to them. They are acting under the influence of the psychological equivalent of the physical law of inertia.

Things in motion tend to remain in motion, and things at rest tend to remain at rest. That is the law of inertia you learned about if you ever took a high school or college physics course. When applied to human behavior, this law explains why anyone who faces the prospect of change initially looks for ways to avoid going through with it. Our natural inclination in almost any situation is to remain the same. We instinctively try to maintain the status quo even when the status quo clearly is not doing us a bit of good.

If you have a chronic case of the blues, this universal tendency is more pronounced because inertia is a symptom of the blues as well as a barrier to overcoming them. Plagued by a pervasive sense of helplessness and hopelessness, you have little faith in your ability to change. The way things are, while not the way you wish they were, are at least familiar. When you wake up in a blue mood, you can predict with reasonable accuracy what the rest of your day will be like, and you know how to handle that. You may not like it, you may complain about it, but it is not nearly as distressing as the prospect of changing course and traveling through unfamiliar territory. And it seems to require less effort or energy than getting off dead center and doing something to overcome the blues.

In addition, because you tend to blame your blue moods on external forces that are beyond your control, you also tend to wait for external circumstances to change or for someone to come along and make you happy. "I know I would cheer up if I was in a steady relationship" is the refrain of many unattached DD sufferers. Danielle echoed it before she met Greg. They have been together for two years now, and Danielle has not "cheered up" yet. "Once tax season is over, I'll feel better" thought Matthew, an accountant. But five tax seasons have come and gone without bringing any noticeable improvement. Chances are that whatever you have pegged as your miracle cure has not miraculously cured you either.

Just as the blues do not come out of nowhere, they will not go away by themselves no matter how much you wish they would. To get relief from the blues, you have to take an active role, push past the inertia that accompanies DD, and overcome one or more of the following forms of resistance as well.

Denying the Reality of the Problem. "Yeah, but . . . it's not that bad (or it could be worse)." When you say this about something that is making you miserable, you are minimizing or denying reality. You are making the ultimate excuse: Since this isn't really a problem (or an important problem or as bad a problem as it could be), I don't have to do anything to solve it.

From the outside looking in, this pretense seems senseless. Why would anyone pretend not to be in pain when acknowledging the truth could lead them to something that would end the pain? Yet, as irrational as it may seem, people deny, minimize, and explain away reality every day. Alcoholics do it. "I'm just a social drinker" or "I only drink beer," they say, as if either fact conclusively proves that they are not dependent on alcohol. Battered spouses do it: "It doesn't happen that often. He feels terrible about it afterward. He never lays a hand on the kids." As if making these statements justifies remaining in an abusive relationship. The woman who finds a lump in her breast tells herself that it's nothing and does not go to the doctor. The employee who learns that his company will be conducting massive layoffs tells himself, "I'm a loyal employee, they'd never let me go" and is shocked when he gets his pink slip.

Why do people do these things, and specifically, why do DD sufferers, who are so obviously hurting and who so often complain about their depressed condition, suddenly play it down when the time comes to take action? The reason is to avoid change but also to protect themselves from yet another blow to their self-esteem. They believe that by admitting they have a problem (especially one like depression, which they think only crybabies or wimps get), they may also be admitting they are flawed, weak-willed, and inept. Such an admission hurts, but if the problem is "not so bad," *they* might not be either—and this premise enables them to "save face."

You are most likely to pursue that line of thinking if you have bought into the myth of self-reliance and the assumption that you should be able to "go it alone," "tough it out," "be a man about it," or any of a dozen other virtuous phrases that in this instance are not virtuous at all. No matter how appropriate they may be in other situations and no matter how often they were drummed into you during childhood, those "shoulds" and "ought to"s are useless if they do not enhance your life in some way. And they definitely do not when it comes to fighting depression. Playing down the magnitude of your problem does not prove that you are strong or self-sufficient. It simply holds you back and guarantees that you do not consider, much less pursue, the alternatives that could help you beat the blues.

Pessimism. "Yeah, but . . . it won't work." This is your depression talking, or more precisely, the pessimism that comes along with any chronic case of the blues. When you have been down in the dumps day in and day out for years, you become absolutely convinced that nothing can help you feel better and that conviction fogs the lens through which you view any alternative suggested to you. You cannot see *how* the new approach could work, so you decide that it will not. And having come to that conclusion, you feel there's no point in trying the potential solution and therefore you keep the problem.

If you are ever to overcome DD, you will have to suspend your disbelief and give therapy or self-help measures a try, acting as if they could work long enough to learn that they really do.

Fear. "Yeah, but . . . it won't work *for me* (nothing has before)." Before you can understand this form of resistance, you need to decode it. When you say, "Sure, that might work for someone else, but it won't work for me" or "I've tried, but nothing has worked for me yet," there is another, more powerful message hidden between the lines: "I can't try what you're suggesting because if I do, I might fail, be disappointed, make a fool of myself, get worse instead of better," and so on. The obstacle you have encountered is fear.

A certain amount of fear, anxiety, and self-doubt is natural and largely unavoidable whenever you are called upon to break an old habit, master a new behavior pattern, or take on any one of the myriad challenges that come your way over the course of your lifetime. Everyone feels fear: the stand-up comedian who is afraid of failing onstage, the platform diver who knows that even a slight miscalculation can be fatal, the housewife reentering the job market, the dysthymic facing change. No one is immune, but some of us feel fear and surge ahead in spite of it, while others let fear stop them in their tracks. If that has happened to you, then you are likely to resist change with a vengeance even though doing so means that you will stay depressed.

Perhaps you fear failure. Already viewing yourself as hopelessly inept, you may equate trying something new with setting yourself up for another failure. Since you do not need any more evidence of your own inadequacy, you do not try. Fear of being disappointed may dog you as well. You don't want to get your hopes up only to discover that you are back down in the dumps again. That would make you feel worse than ever. Fear of success sometimes rears its ugly head too. What if your mysterious blue mood should lift but your life is still a mess, your marriage is still on the rocks, your job is still boring, your children are still unruly and unappreciative? What would be the point of feeling better then? Finally, fear of the unknown is perhaps the most pervasive fear of them all. As was mentioned earlier, the hell you know is at least familiar and often seems better than the uncharted landscape you would enter if you actually changed. The fact of the matter is that change, even life itself, is a risky business. It involves taking chances, possibly failing, possibly embarrassing yourself, possibly being disappointed, and possibly becoming painfully aware of your own limitations.

Yet taking chances also means possibly succeeding, possibly feeling proud of yourself, possibly having things turn out the way you hoped they would, and possibly becoming joyfully aware of your own strengths and positive attributes. Because you have been bogged down by a chronic case of the blues and focusing on all you stand to lose, you have probably forgotten that there are potential gains from taking risks. Now is the perfect time to remember that by trying to be completely safe, by refusing all challenges and declining all invitations, you eliminate all opportunities for happiness. But by pushing past your fears, by acknowledging them and then taking risks anyway, health, pleasure, and a life unburdened by a chronic case of the blues becomes possible again.

Lack of Energy. "Yeah, but . . . I don't have the energy." You may not realize how much of your energy goes into fueling and maintaining your depression. You consume enormous amounts of energy and time ruminating about your sad state of affairs, berating yourself for your perceived failures and inadequacies, conjuring up worst-case scenarios for the future, stifling your anger or resentment, and engaging in a wide range of self-defeating behaviors.

In addition, because you are depressed, you are likely to view everything as a chore that saps your strength. Yet, as any nondepressed person can tell you (and you, too, can discover), many activities that seem burdensome at first actually lift your spirits and energize you.

Perfectionism. "Yeah, but . . . I'm still not sure this is the right approach for me (or the right time to try it)." Right or wrong is not the issue here. Perfectionism is. When you experience this form of resistance, your extreme desire to find the perfect solution to your problems and execute it flawlessly can actually lead you to do nothing at all.

You start this self-defeating cycle by wanting to overcome the blues in one fell swoop, without any delays, errors, or setbacks. That's perfectionism—and chances are that you already apply it to other areas of your life, as Andrea did. She was a typical perfection seeker, wanting a perfect job, a perfect relationship, a perfect social life, a perfect figure, self-image, and mood. But most of all she wanted to find the perfect moment to change, one when all the other pieces of her life were in perfect order and she had found a self-improvement measure that came with an ironclad, money-back guarantee. She was willing—indeed, she seemed determined—to wait until that moment arrived. That's procrastination.

Like Andrea, you have had far more practice coming up with excuses not to act than experience acting on your own behalf. Indeed, your sophisticated fault-finding mechanism can identify a drawback to any self-improvement plan, a problem with any moment in time, and a troublesome external condition that stands between you and any positive step you can take. Aiming for perfection while at the same time being a true genius at spotting imperfections enables you to procrastinate for a long, long time.

Unfortunately, the longer you put something off, the larger and more difficult the task becomes. A rut becomes a deep, dark hole and then a canyon with walls a mile high. Once you simply could have stepped out of the rut, but now scaling those canyon walls seems to be completely beyond your capabilities. It's overwhelming, it's impossible, you cannot do it, you cannot do anything, you are paralyzed. And once paralysis sets in, it practically takes a stick of dynamite to get you moving in a positive direction again.

To overcome this form of resistance, start by facing the fact that perfection is unattainable, then lower your standards. By this I do not mean accepting that you will never be happy or settling for whatever fate sends your way. I do mean aiming for excellence—the best you can do or be at any given moment—even though, at that moment, the actual circumstances of your life may place certain limitations on you. While you have been waiting for those restrictive circumstances to disappear and for perfect moments, conditions, or solutions to appear in their place, life and many excellent but imperfect opportunities have been passing you by.

You also lower your standards in a healthy way when you take the advice that twelve-step recovery programs such as Alcoholics Anonymous offer their members—strive for *progress*, not perfection. When you can get through one day (or one hour) without feeling blue or when you can encounter one stressful situation without drawing unproductive conclusions about it, you have made progress toward getting better. Focusing on that fact rather than on how blue you still are or how much further you have to go will motivate you to keep moving forward.

BENEFITS OF THE BLUES

Sooner or later, however, you simply have to take the plunge. After all . . . what do you have to lose? This is more than a rhetorical question, and it is probably a familiar one for those of you who have been down in the dumps for an extended period of time. It is part of the logical argument you so often hear from people who want to help you. "If you feel rotten and something can make you feel better, why not try it? What do you have to lose?" they ask. In addition to all of the rationalizations your inertia and resistance to change supply as answers to that question, there is one that you may not even be aware of. You *do* have something to lose: the benefits or "secondary gains" you get from enduring circumstances that are mostly negative for you. In a roundabout way DD gives you something that you need and may not know how to get in any other way. This concept is difficult to grasp and even more difficult to swallow. How can anyone obtain anything of value from a chronic case of the blues? What on earth can be so positively reinforcing that someone would put up with all the painful symptoms of DD and keep putting up with them even after they knew how to relieve those symptoms? Perhaps something Danielle mentioned during one of her interviews will give you a clue.

"I became an artist because I had a talent in that area," Danielle explained, "but there was more to it than that. When I was still rather young, I realized I had the temperament for it. I had the same intensity, the same moodiness, the same demons as the great artists I read about. I understood how they felt. I identified with their struggles to find and create beauty in a disappointing, downright depressing world."

Although all artists are not prone to depression, the ones Danielle read about were, and she came to think of them as kindred spirits, role models who shared her worldview or, in this instance, her blue mood mind-set. Their biographies made an indelible impression on Danielle, showing her that other people not only felt the way she did but also did something with those feelings. They created art. Danielle, who already enjoyed artistic endeavors and had a great deal of natural artistic ability, decided she would too. In addition to enabling her to pursue something at which she could excel, this choice also provided Danielle with an explanation for her blue moods. They were part of her "artistic temperament."

In this way, she actually utilized her depression toward a productive goal. Ultimately, though, this survival skill did not serve her well. For Danielle, her art became so identified with her depression that as time went on she unwittingly found herself reluctant to let go of her blue moods.

FACTS ABOUT DD

In evaluating your relationship with depression, it is easy to rationalize a course of no action. Instead, consider these facts:

Fact: Doing nothing is the surest way to stay depressed—and it may worsen your depression.

While your chances of magically getting better by doing nothing are almost nil, your chances of getting worse are significant. For more than one-third of all DD sufferers, an untended case of dysthymia leads to a major depressive episode.

Fact: Something will work for you.

None of the people I interviewed had any faith in their ability to overcome DD, yet most of them and all of the individuals you have read about thus far did get better once they made an effort on their own behalf. All of them did not beat the blues in the same way, not everything they tried worked for them, but something did and something will work for you too. For some of you, the self-help strategies in the next four chapters will be enough. For others, this will only be a starting point, and therapy or a combination of therapy and antidepressant medication will bring about more dramatic results. No matter how you go about it, if you genuinely want to feel better and you work at getting better, you will.

Fact: It won't be easy.

If you are still thinking that it's not that easy, you are right. Change is never easy, and when you are depressed it is even more difficult. Every aspect of the blues conspires to keep you in the same old dragged out, helpless, hopeless, depressed condition. But keep in mind that taking the easy route is how you got where you are today. If you really want to stay where you are (or slide further downhill), you can give in to your depression and give up. No one can make you change. If you want to be someplace else, however, you will have to do things differently from the way you have in the past, even if doing so isn't easy.

Fact: Doing *anything* is better than doing nothing.

If doing nothing will keep you down in the dumps, it doesn't take a rocket scientist to figure out that doing something is better than doing nothing. Aside from the fact that the following exercises have proven helpful for others, there is also something to be said for simply making an effort. For nearly every dysthymic, just taking action—regardless of the action taken—has a noticeably uplifting effect.

One last fact: Help is available.

If you are mired in a swamp of negativity, if you feel so hopeless and exhausted that despite your desire to feel better you cannot bring yourself to try any of the self-help measures, please consider the alternative of getting professional help now. A mental health professional can provide the objective assessment of your condition that you may need as well as guide you through a recovery process that seems too complicated or difficult to pursue on your own.

APPROACHES TO OVERCOMING DD

With the above facts in mind, read through the next three chapters. Each tackles one additional aspect of the four-pronged approach to overcoming DD that parallels the components of a blue mood (emotional, cognitive, behavioral, and interpersonal). Although you eventually will want to work on all these areas, it is best to pick the one you are most engaged by to start. Proceed with the others in any order.

Give the strategies a chance. Although you may react to what you read with skepticism and feel tempted to find loopholes in the advice, select your starting point and see your way through chapters five through eight. It helps tremendously to view the self-help program in the chapter you picked not as a surefire cure for all that ails you but, instead, as an experiment, a project you are undertaking to see if you can have an impact on your blue mood.

For most of you, feeling better will take practice and time to uncover unproductive thinking or uproot self-defeating habits, and it will take repetition to make new thought and behavior patterns stick. Doing each exercise once will not be enough. You need to keep using them and working them into the tapestry of your life. Although some of the suggestions pertain to routines and positive habits, you will want to continue indefinitely. To get started, make a one-month commitment and stick to it even if you do not notice immediate, dramatic results.

Continue rating your mood and energy levels on the Self-Monitoring Chart found in chapter four. Evaluate your progress at the end of the month (not before). Remember that you are aiming for improvement, not perfection. If you give these strategies your best attempt, you *will* see that improvement.

6

Cognitive Switches: Unproductive Thinking

Remember Beverly, the bank teller and divorced mother of two who thought herself into a blue mood over what was supposed to be an enjoyable lunch? Well, she did it again on a recent Saturday afternoon. She was in the middle of doing a week's worth of laundry and baking six apple pies for the church bake sale when her teenage daughters announced that she *had to* drive them to the mall where they had arranged to meet their friends. Already "racing around like a chicken with its head cut off" and annoyed that they had not consulted her before making plans that involved her, Beverly not only refused to be their "personal chauffeur" but also listed all the other ways they took advantage of her. Then she told her daughters that if they wanted to go to the mall so badly, they could walk the eight blocks to the bus stop and take the bus.

As they stormed out of the house, slamming the front door behind them, Beverly thought, "What's the matter with me? I shouldn't have said those things. I should have controlled my temper." In an attempt to justify her actions (and assuage her guilt), she told herself that "if they weren't so selfish and self-centered, this never would have happened." But whose fault is that? she asked herself. Hers, she decided. "If I had raised them right to begin with, they would have compassion for other people now," she thought, labeling herself a "lousy" parent. Soon she was comparing herself to her sister and reminding herself that "Amanda never has problems with her kids."

From the moment she began telling herself what she should and should not have done, Beverly was in trouble. She was engaging in dysfunctional or unproductive thinking. Once such thinking starts, it generally keeps rolling. Thus, without meaning to, Beverly played a game of "Can You Top This?" with herself, conjuring up one disturbing idea after another until their combined weight all but crushed her. Then, as most unproductive thinkers do, Beverly went one step further: She allowed her runaway thoughts to dictate her actions.

Already feeling completely inadequate and unbearably guilty, it suddenly occurred to Beverly that she would feel even worse if "something horrible" happened to her daughters en route to the mall. Conjuring up images of a gang of knife-wielding thugs accosting her children on their way to the bus stop, she grabbed her car keys, raced out of the house, intercepted her daughters, and not only drove them to the mall but insisted that they call her for a ride home instead of getting a lift from their friend's mother.

In addition to all the misery her guilt-inducing "shoulds" and self-criticism caused her, by doing what she did Beverly managed to add more items to her schedule—and by playing "catch-up," she felt overwhelmed for the rest of the day. Unable to get to everything she planned to do, Beverly hit herself with another barrage of "shoulds" and self-criticism, convincing herself that she really was hopelessly disorganized and inept.

To grasp what happened to Beverly, imagine what would happen if she was the manager of a company and she constantly criticized her staff and never praised them; told them they would fail each time she assigned them a task; reminded them of all their previous mistakes each time they made the slightest error; and at every opportunity called them losers, idiots, or hopeless, powerless victims. In other words, what would the outcome be if Beverly treated her employees the way she treated herself? The result would be an unhappy, unhealthy, unproductive staff. Your chronic case of the blues stems in large measure from this same sort of mismanagement and can be relieved by developing and *using* the new thought-management skills you will learn about in this chapter.

UNPRODUCTIVE THOUGHT PATTERNS

Whether you pile one unproductive idea on top of another or spring into action because of them, you are managing your thoughts in a way that virtually guarantees your blues will not go away. But as previously mentioned, you may not know you are doing that. Thinking yourself into a blue mood tends to be an automatic response, a reflex reaction to everyday events and situations that expose the areas where you are already plagued with self-doubts or memories of past negative experiences. Like nail biting, hair twirling, pencil tapping, or any other repeated motions, your self-defeating thought patterns are habits, mental habits. And like other habits, they can be broken. As a very effective treatment for depression, cognitive therapy has demonstrated time and again, if your thought patterns are impaired, you *can* change them.

According to Rational-Emotive therapist Albert Ellis, your thoughts are what carry you from point A (a stressful or upsetting event) to point C (an unsettling or painful emotional state). Just as you can prevent an explosion by cutting the fuse that runs between a spark and a stick of dynamite, if you train yourself to fill in the B and practice retracing the path your thoughts traveled, you can learn to spot unproductive thoughts while you are thinking them and prevent new bouts of the blues. Ellis developed a process to help his patients get started and called it the ABC technique. Here is what happened when Joel tried it.

Joel had been feeling anxious all day. In fact, at one point his chest felt so tight that he feared he was on the brink of a heart attack and canceled his weekly racquetball game. As usual, he thought his emotional state had just happened. After all, he had been "keyed up" from the moment he had awoken that morning. Nothing unusual happened, he insisted: "The radio alarm clock went off at the usual time. A commercial was just ending, and the news announcer came on, gave the date, and made some comment about income tax day being right around the corner."

Joel abruptly stopped speaking. He had found point A. The radio announcer's reference to income taxes had reminded Joel that he had not prepared his tax return yet and that was where his chain of thought began. Hoping to motivate himself to get his tax return done, he gave himself a mini-lecture, and while he was at it, he rebuked himself about a half-dozen other areas he had been neglecting: cleaning his untidy apartment, replacing the threadbare tires on his car, updating his lesson plans, doing something about his social life and his life in general. Unintentionally he had taken the need to complete one task, turned it into an impossibly crowded agenda, and concluded that "everything was totally out of control," that he "was on the verge of falling apart completely." Believing that, who wouldn't feel anxious?

Now you try it. *Start by identifying point A and point C.* Since Joel knew he felt anxious but did not know why, he started at point C and worked backward to pinpoint when he began feeling that way and what was happening at that time. You can do that too. Recall a recent time when you felt upset, identify your exact feelings, and review the events that came before the feelings until you find the one that probably triggered them. Or you can start at point A, identifying a recent stressful event, and then recall how you felt about it.

Then, *fill in point B:* Ask yourself the following questions:

What did the event mean to me?

What did I tell myself during and after it?

What was I expecting to happen that didn't, or what wasn't I expecting that did happen? What did that mean to me?

Did this situation remind me of something that had happened to me before and turned out poorly? Did it push a button or hit a sore spot?

After you have developed a general idea of what you were thinking, *write down in your notebook your train of thought, replicating the sequence of ideas as closely as you can* (that is, what you thought first, second, third, and so on).

The first time you read these instructions, you may think they are asking the impossible, and the first time you try to follow them, you may indeed discover that uncovering your hidden thought patterns presents quite a challenge. Be assured that the ABC technique gets easier with practice and that practicing it is worth the effort. First, you can use it to explain any emotional state that baffles you and the blue moods that seem to "just happen" to you. Just realizing that you are not at the mercy of mysterious external forces will provide some relief. Second, it enables you to move from tracking your thoughts after the fact to paying attention to the thoughts you are thinking while you are thinking them. And finally, it helps you recognize the *types* of unproductive thoughts that repeatedly bring on or intensify the blues. Once you have identified those habits and cognitive glitches, you can begin figuring out why they are defeating you—and then do something to correct them.

UNREALISTIC AND INACCURATE THOUGHTS

Whether they are hidden or clearly visible in the things you say to yourself and other people, your thoughts are persuasive. They can also be unreasonable, distorted, or unfair to yourself and other people. Indeed, many of your most upsetting, unproductive thoughts may not be accurate or realistic at all.

Susan, an officer on a large urban police force, failed the sergeant's exam on her first try. So did 50 percent of the other officers who took it. Some acknowledged that they had not really studied for it. Some of them said it was harder than they'd expected and said that before taking it again they would have to study harder, concentrating on the subjects they had not realized would be on the test. Still others admitted that they were so nervous their minds went blank. Next time around they would know what they were facing and be more relaxed. In contrast, Susan was well on her way to deciding that for her there would be no next time. Although she thought she would make a good sergeant, she was convinced that the test was biased, put together by and for the white male officers who traditionally dominated the force. She resented having to take a test that didn't measure her true capabilities and believed that the "deck was stacked against her."

Telling herself that women will never truly be accepted on the force, she decided that she "didn't stand a chance of succeeding" and concluded that "there is really no point in trying. I might as well give up." Months after the sergeant's exam she was still walking around with a king-sized chip on her shoulder and spending her nonworking hours stewing bitterly over "the unfairness of it all." The next time the test was given, Susan did not take it, and she is now thinking about putting in for a desk job where she can do enough to get by and no more.

Since Susan's thoughts created resentment and despair, adversely affected her job performance, and prevented her from achieving her original goals, they were clearly unproductive. As you will see, they were also inaccurate and in some instances false.

Since many tests have proved to be biased, Susan's first thought that the sergeant's exam was biased and unfair may have been accurate. She also may have been right about its being biased and unfair toward women. However, by focusing on that bias and overlooking the possibility that the test might not fairly measure the capabilities of other minorities, Susan was singling herself out as a victim and deducing that since she was a woman, the test was unfair to her personally. This distortion added an extra jolt of emotion to an already upsetting situation.

At this point Susan could have told herself: "I want to be a sergeant, and to do that I must pass the test even if it is biased and unfair. If I study harder and pass the test as well as perform my job even better than I have in the past, I can get what I want." Unfortunately, that was not what Susan did. Rather than looking for ways to overcome the obstacle she had encountered, Susan's unproductive thinking prepared her to surrender to it.

When Susan thought that women would never truly be accepted in the department, she extended her perception of bias and unfair treatment to include the entire police force, discounting the many members of the department who were actually neutral on the matter of female police officers, not to mention all the individuals who had offered her their encouragement and support. Then she concluded that because she was a woman, she didn't stand a chance of succeeding. Not only did this negate the irrefutable fact that there were a number of women who *had* succeeded in becoming sergeants and several who had advanced even further, but it also predicted failure based on something that was beyond Susan's control: her gender. Although it was patently untrue, Susan nonetheless assumed that her assessment was accurate and acted accordingly. She gave up her dreams and stopped trying to succeed.

If Susan had instead examined her thoughts and tested their validity, she might have spared herself a painful downhill slide. It rarely occurs to many of us to question our thoughts or consider alternative explanations for our experiences. And as a result the same unproductive thoughts are apt to carry us down the same path to the same destination. For DD sufferers that destination is almost always the conclusion that the situation is hopeless and they are powerless to change it, and this causes their depression. As you know, that thinking is precisely what keeps a chronic case of the blues alive.

To change course and overcome the blues, you must learn to view your thoughts not as facts but as hypotheses, theories that may or may not be valid. Before you accept these hypotheses as truth or act upon them, you must test them and, if they prove to be invalid, correct them. You accomplish this feat by familiarizing yourself with the early warning signs of unproductive thinking and then refuting, revising, or replacing those thoughts by using the strategies given below.

NEGATIVE AND DISTORTED THINKING

While Susan's thoughts were unproductive and inaccurate, the same could not be said for Kevin, an unemployed advertising executive in his mid-forties. As he frequently reminded me, he had *real* problems. When his company lost a major account, Kevin lost his job, and he quickly learned there was not a huge demand for middle-aged executives who wanted salaries commensurate with their years of professional experience. "I've been out of work for nine months now," he said. "I've gone on interview after interview only to see young, inexperienced upstarts get jobs that I could do with ease. If I don't catch up on my mortgage payments soon, I'm going to lose my house, and my wife rarely misses an opportunity to remind me that she is supporting us now. So don't tell me my problems are all in my head." Kevin was right. His problems were real. He was not fantasizing or exaggerating reality. Yet by constantly counting the days he had been without a job, the dollars left in his savings account, and the number of times he had been interviewed, he was thinking every bit as unproductively as someone who makes decisions based on inaccurate assumptions. He was still holding himself back and keeping himself down in the dumps.

Like many DD sufferers, Kevin processed information selectively, concentrating on one aspect of a situation (usually the most negative one) and then re-creating or exaggerating it in a way that gave him ample opportunity to be depressed. I call this type of unproductive thinking "looking through a negativity lens." You may do it by perpetually pondering upsetting facts and unpleasant realities the way Kevin did, or you may discount the positive side of any situation and focus only on the down side (which you have probably exaggerated).

For instance, Ed had intended to retire at sixty-five. Indeed, he had looked forward to it, judiciously saving his money and joyfully planning for his sunset years. Then when he was sixty-two, the company where he had worked throughout his career was taken over by another company, and Ed was forced into early retirement. Since he was given a substantial severance payment that ensured he would not suffer financially, Ed might have looked at this turn of events as a golden opportunity to realize his plans for the future sooner than he had expected. But Ed did not see it that way. Looking at the situation through a negativity lens, Ed saw unappreciative employers "putting him out to pasture" and conveying to him that he was not a good worker or a valued member of the corporation. Mulling this over, Ed sank slowly into the quicksand of the blues.

When you suffer from this same sort of psychological tunnel vision, you are drawn to sad stories, the unpleasant features of any encounter, and all evidence of your own shortcomings like a magnet. When anything goes wrong, you run instant replays of the "disaster" all day long. Like the throbbing of a painful paper cut, any unkind word, any bit of criticism lingers in your mind and can erase twenty-four hours' worth of positive comments from your memory bank. You tune out the positive things in life, minimizing their importance or failing to notice them at all.

Another Friday night alone, Joel thought as he entered a local shopping arcade and glumly headed for the video store. In his mind he could see the empty hours that lay ahead and wished that he had a girlfriend to watch a vintage video with him or go out with him for a candlelit dinner in a romantic setting. Shuffling along with his shoulders hunched forward and his gaze directed downward, Joel did not notice the attractive woman by the jewelry cart who definitely noticed him. He was oblivious to the pretty young clerk in the bookstore who recognized him and tried to catch his eye. When he did look up, Joel saw only couples, families, and groups of teens with their friends. "Everybody has someone," he thought morosely, "except me."

As you can see, a negativity lens not only focuses on the depressing side of any story, it also filters out all positive feelings, experiences, and possibilities. While looking through it you are so hypersensitive to any hint of potential criticism or rejection that you can transform even neutral experiences into negative ones. For example, if three of your friends compliment your cooking and a fourth does not, you wonder why he said nothing and worry about what he thought. Or if you call about a recent job interview and are told the final decision has not yet been made, you hear "coldness" in the interviewer's voice and think it means that you have been rejected already.

Because your mental filtering system ensures that your concept of everything that happens to you is consistent with what you already believe about yourself, the world, and your future, no new light can be shed on any problem, no positive data about yourself can get through to you. Your problems do not get solved, and you maintain your negative self-image and sustain your chronic case of the blues.

Early Warning Signals. Here are several early warning signals that can alert you to the fact that you are interpreting your experiences from a distorted, blue point of view.

If only . . . , I wish . . . : Both of these phrases are sure signs that your thoughts are focused on something that you do *not* have. It may be a condition that cannot be met. "If only I had my old job back," Kevin moaned. "If only I had not been fired . . ." But of course he had been, and there was no way he could alter that fact. On the other hand, Joel focused on something he could obtain. He wished he had a girlfriend, but aside from wishing, griping about being alone, and convincing himself that he was the only male in the entire city of San Francisco who did not "have someone," Joel did nothing to get what he wanted. Chances are that if you too have thoughts filled with "I wish" and "if only," neither will you. While training your gaze on the down side, you cannot see what you do have going for you or the options for change that are available to you.

Yeah, but . . . : As discussed in detail in the last chapter, when this phrase appears in your thoughts or conversations, you are filtering out positive possibilities. Your fault-finding mechanism is on maximum over-drive, prompting you to veto any suggestion before thinking it through or to conclude that negative outcomes are preordained. As a result you unwittingly sentence yourself to do more time in the prison of your chronic blue mood.

What was that really about? What was he or she really trying to tell me? These two questions let you know that you are honing in on the possible hidden agendas and ulterior motives in other people's words and actions. Most people manipulate, beat around the bush, or otherwise camouflage their real thoughts and feelings every once in a while, but some people do it frequently. The trouble is that while viewing life through a nega-tivity lens, you suspect almost everyone of doing it most of the time, along with assuming that the hidden message is a negative commentary on you. Thus, if your boss stops by your desk as you are preparing to leave work on a Friday afternoon and says, "Glad I caught you. I'd like you to stop by my office first thing Monday morning to discuss the Miller report," you might think, "Why did she say she caught me? Was I leaving too early? Does she think I've been slacking off lately? Maybe that's the real reason she wants to see me." By filling in the imaginary blanks in this manner, you have just bought yourself a ticket for a weekend-long ride on the blue mood merry-go-round.

If they only knew . . . It's only a matter of time until he/she finds out . . . I'm a fraud and am in danger of being unmasked because . . . When these phrases and feelings surface, you can bet that you have just en-countered someone or something that is inconsistent with your blue mood mind-set. You are having a positive experience that just seems unearned. Most typically, someone is treating you better than you think you deserve to be treated or seems to see you in a more positive light than you see yourself. That was precisely what happened to Judy when Pete, the attractive man she met at her co-worker's birthday party, invited her to a Cubs game and she bolted for the bathroom.

As you may recall, Judy considered herself unattractive, dull, and boring. Indeed, she was so convinced of this that when she attracted favorable attention, she felt like a fraud. The only reason anyone would be attentive to someone as dull and boring as she was that she had "conned" them into thinking she was interesting and appealing. Like a child about to be caught with her hand in the cookie jar, Judy's supposed deception stirred up feelings of guilt and anxiety. After all, it was only a matter of time until the man with whom she was conversing discovered what she knew to be true, and once he "saw through her," he would reject her—an assumption that caused her to panic and run. It also robbed her of a positive experience that might have relieved her blue mood.

Focus on the Positive. Where you focus your attention is your choice. The lens through which you view life is selected by you. Although the negativity lens is apt to be the only one you have used in recent years, it is not the only one available. It will take time, practice, and at first very small adjustments to change your focus. You will not be able to "just look on the bright side," as people have so often encouraged you to do. Instead, you must train yourself to be aware of positive signs and to pay more attention to the positive feedback you receive from other people, your positive accomplishments, and so on. To do this, you should keep a "positive experiences" diary.

Obtain a pocket-size notebook, one that is small enough to carry with you wherever you go. In it, record everything positive that you experience, notice, hear from other people, and accomplish. Everything—meaning whatever is not negative. Include things you accomplish that you might tend to take for granted (getting out of bed, getting dressed, driving on the freeway without having an accident, and so forth). It does not matter that you might have been able to do something better or sooner. If you did it, write it down.

Record any positive comments made to you, compliments paid to you, or respectful treatment given to you. Positives you may not have appreciated lately include courteous salesclerks, people who held doors open for you, the words "thank you."

Identify at least two positive aspects of your appearance daily. You do not have to be positively gorgeous or the next Arnold Schwarzenegger. If your socks match, your hair is clean, your earrings are attractive, then write it down.

Finally, each day try to notice ten positives in the world around you—a news story about a medical breakthrough or a fund-raising event, children playing together, the first crocus of spring, someone helping an elderly person carry groceries down the street. If you look for these things, you will find them. Either before you go to bed or when you wake up, read your journal entries to remind yourself that good things do happen.

Please note that this refocusing exercise is not asking you to ignore the fact that negative things also happen. You do not need any practice spotting them. What you need is to practice seeing the whole picture and an opportunity to develop a broader, more balanced view of yourself and the world in which you live. This exercise enables you to do that. Your holistic perspective will become as natural as your negative one once was. This exercise may seem tedious, but if you keep track of your positive experiences faithfully for at least a month, you surely will notice a marked improvement in your overall mood. So try it.

UNREASONABLE, UNREALISTIC, OR RIGID RULES

If you have ever watched a TV police show or worked for a bureaucracy, you have heard the phrase "going by the book." It is used to describe someone who makes every decision based on rigid, one-size-fits-all rules and regulations that can either be found in a procedural manual or that represent "the way it has always been done around here." Someone who goes by the book makes no exceptions, no allowances for extenuating circumstances, and no room for human error or differences of opinion. He or she shows no mercy for anyone who breaks or bends even the most arbitrary rule. Neither do you if you have established unreasonable, unrealistic, or excessively rigid rules that you expect yourself and everyone else to live by.

The rules to which I am referring are not necessarily laws or codes of ethics or even societal norms to which large groups subscribe. They are your own personal, deeply ingrained beliefs about what is or is not a good, right, or acceptable way to think, feel, or behave. Those standards have the potential to guide you through the rocky terrain of daily living, but if they are too absolute, arbitrary, inflexible, or extreme, your rules will defeat *you* instead.

How can you tell if this is happening to you? Here are some telltale words or phrases and the effect they can have on you.

Should: You enroll in an adult education course for the challenge of learning something new, but every time the teacher calls on you, it feels as if you are facing a firing squad. No matter what the question, you *should* know the answer, you think. And if you do not, you *should not* be in the class.

You are a single parent and believe that you must be both mother and father to your three young sons. Consequently, you hold down a full-time job, run your household, and run yourself ragged taking your boys to sporting events and on camping trips as well as being a den mother for their scout troop.

Your neighbors are inconsiderate bores who have a habit of dropping by at dinnertime, mooching a meal, and hanging around until late at night. One minute you tell yourself that you *should* be more assertive and set some limits on them, but the next you are rebuking yourself for having such a thought. You *ought to* be more patient and understanding, you think. Either way you are miserable.

The word *should* and its close relatives *must* and *ought to* are gateways to self-criticism and sure signs that you are trying to "whip" yourself into shape, to prod yourself into measuring up to some lofty and usually unattainable standard you have set for yourself. When plagued by this type of unreasonable thinking, you find that there is never an end in sight no matter how much you accomplish. There are always more "should"s waiting in the wings.

Many of them are extreme and absolute. For instance, you may believe that you should be kind and considerate *no matter what,* succeed at *everything* you do, be liked by *everyone* you meet, *never* make mistakes, or be in control of your emotions *at all times*. No one could actually live up to such high standards, but you expect it of yourself and rarely give yourself a break. Each time you think you have done something you should not do or not done something that you should, you have broken a rule and the path is clear: You must be punished, you must feel bad—indeed, you do not deserve to feel good.

What are some of your "should"s? In your notebook jot down any that came to mind while you were reading this section or that appeared in the thoughts you had while using the ABC technique. Underline those that involve extremes.

When I . . . then I will . . . In order to . . . I must . . . : People who go by the book frequently put a price tag on happiness. Your "procedural manual" states in no uncertain terms that you must earn the right to be happy or achieve specific goals before you can enjoy life. When you lose ten pounds, then you will be happy, you think. You believe that in order to feel good about yourself you must be in a relationship or that you would feel fulfilled and satisfied with your life if you had a better job. The rule itself is not as defeating as its implication—that you cannot be happy until you lose ten pounds, that you cannot feel good about yourself unless you are in a relationship, or that it is impossible for you to feel fulfilled and satisfied without getting a better job. If you were to feel happy, worthwhile, or satisfied without those things, you would be breaking the rules (and would lose your right to feel good). Scary, isn't it? Yet that is precisely the bind people with chronic cases of the blues put themselves in.

Identify any of your rules that fit the above description and write them in your notebook.

He/she/they should . . . : When you harbor thoughts such as, "He should have known that would upset me," "She should understand that I'm too depressed to get involved with her charity fund-raiser," or "They should not be taking advantage of me this way," you are projecting your expectations onto other people and assuming that they know what your rules are and have agreed to adhere to them. At the very least this misconception will lead to countless misunderstandings. It often turns minor conflicts into raging battles and can leave you endlessly outraged and indignant.

List the rules you expect other people to live by, especially those "he/she/they should" thoughts that seem to crop up repeatedly.

It's not fair . . . I can't believe this is happening (or why is this happening) . . . : These phrases tell you that life in general and events occurring in the world around you are not "going by the book"—or not your book anyway. The unexpected has happened. Someone who wants to pay by check but can't find her courtesy card is tying up the express lane at the grocery store. Construction on the freeway has traffic backed up for miles. Your regular babysitter comes down with the flu. Things just aren't going according to plan, and your "procedural manual" says not only that they must but that it is catastrophic when they do not. Consequently, you fall apart at the seams or dismally declare, "Now my entire day is ruined"—which is, by the way, yet another indication that you are thinking unproductively.

In your notebook specify the things in your life that you label "unfair," events that occur which you cannot believe happen and anything that can "ruin" your entire day.

Reasonable, Realistic, and Flexible Alternatives. The rules you live by defeat you because you try to make reality fit your standards instead of the other way around. When going by the book blocks the path to happiness and repeatedly sends you down the road to despair, it is time to come up with more reasonable, realistic, and flexible alternatives.

1. Take a closer look at the rules you have listed in your notebook. Star those that you cannot help but break because no one could live up to them. For example, no one succeeds at everything they try; people cannot understand how you feel if you do not express your feelings.
2. Place an X in front of any that you apply arbitrarily or indiscriminately, without considering your true circumstances. For instance, in the middle of delicate contract negotiations or while trying to calm a distraught friend, it may be in your best interest to maintain control over your emotions. When you are grieving, however, stifling your feelings in the name of self-control can be harmful; and when you are under pressure or anxious about upcoming events, it is only natural to snap at people, giggle at odd moments, or have tears come to your eyes. You may prefer not to do those things, but doing them is permissible—and forgivable.
3. Place an exclamation point beside rules that are making you miserable. They may or may not fall into either of the previous two categories, but something about them repeatedly gets in your way.
4. Rewrite the rules. Refute or revise them in a way that would eliminate their star, X, or exclamation point status. Here are some examples:

OLD RULE: I should be more efficient.
NEW IDEA: I would like to be more efficient.
OLD RULE: I must get up and prepare a hot breakfast for my children before school each morning.
NEW IDEA: I can get up and prepare a hot breakfast for my children two or three mornings a week.
OLD RULE: I must never lose my temper.
NEW IDEA: I can control my temper. Although I do not intend to and try not to, sometimes I will lose my temper.
OLD RULE: I will be happy when I am earning X number of dollars per year.

NEW IDEA: I can be happy even though I am not yet earning as much money as I someday will.

OLD RULE: When my boss changes his mind about what he wants me to do, it ruins my entire day.

NEW IDEA: When my boss changes his mind, it inconveniences me, but once I have done as he has asked, my day can proceed smoothly.

Once you have rewritten your rules, read and reread them until you have committed them to memory, or make a copy to consult when you catch yourself feeling as if you are not "measuring up." Revise other unproductive rules as you become aware of them.

CANCEL THE GUILT TRIP

Sometimes your view of yourself fuels your sense of inadequacy and powerlessness, sustains your perception of yourself as flawed or undeserving, and leaves you feeling guilty, not good enough, or completely worthless most of the time. Consider the following ways of canceling these guilt trips:

1. Identify something you feel guilty about. Think about something you should have done or don't deserve to have and jot it down.
2. What did you actually do wrong? Answer this question fully. Consider everything you could have done, felt obligated to do, or that a "better person" would have done. Think about the level of performance you expected from yourself, then describe what you did wrong. List the standards you expected yourself to meet in that situation.
3. Were your expectations realistic? Would you make those same demands of a stranger? Did the demands take into consideration the realities of the situation, and were they really your responsibility in the first place? Or were they more like the unreasonable rules you revised earlier? Remember that you are not a god. It is unrealistic to ask of yourself what you would not ask of an ordinary person. With this in mind revise your standards, crossing out anything that was not your responsibility and toning down everything else.
4. Did you meet your revised standards? If you did, cancel the guilt trip. You are berating yourself over something that is more imaginary than reality-based. Of course, since we all make mistakes or do things we later regret, some of you may *not* have lived up to

your revised standards. What then? Apologize, discuss the situation with the other people involved, look for alternatives, and learn new skills for handling similar situations in the future. Or you can apply some of the behavioral techniques found in the next chapter, let yourself off the hook, and move on.

Stopping Unwanted Thoughts. Guilt-ridden thoughts as well as self-critical, self-punishing, and self-pitying ones are persistent little devils, constantly reappearing, intruding at inopportune moments, and triggering yet another downhill slide. The following technique developed by behavioral therapists can help prevent unwanted thoughts. Based on the simple idea that you cannot consciously focus on more than one thought at a time, this technique allows you to derail a negative train of thought by saying or thinking STOP! or visualizing a stop sign when unwanted thoughts come to mind.

Think about a self-defeating or unproductive idea. One of the guilt-ridden ones you identified in the previous strategy would work. Once that thought is clearly in your mind, *imagine yourself yelling STOP! or say it out loud.* Then close your eyes and take a deep breath. You might try visualizing someone or something that makes you feel calm or secure.

Open your eyes and focus your attention on writing a letter, reading a magazine article, doing a household chore, balancing your checkbook, or some other task. *If the unproductive thought returns, start over, beginning with the word* STOP.

The more you practice this technique, the more adept you will become at stopping your thoughts. Eventually, with a softly whispered *stop* or a quickly visualized stop sign, you will be able to (at least temporarily) silence any self-defeating or intrusive thought that comes to mind.

Affirmations. The thought-stopping technique can derail a distressing thought pattern temporarily; however, to ensure that your unproductive ideas do not return to haunt you and that your cognitive glitches do not defeat you, you must replace your old negativity with new, positive, and accurate ideas. These healthy thoughts, deliberately woven into your mind-set to provide comfort, encouragement, and reminders of what you have going for you, are called positive affirmations.

In your notebook, compile a list of twenty (20) positive affirmations. Several have already been suggested in chapter two. You should also find them on the first page of your notebook. Here are a few more possibilities:

1. I can control my mood if I put my mind to it.
2. It is possible to do work I enjoy and get paid for it.
3. I will find a satisfying relationship by actively looking for one and learning what I need to know to be in one.
4. I am open to ideas that might help me to overcome the blues.
5. I am proud of the step I took by picking up and reading this book.

Once your list is made, read your affirmations aloud slowly, listening to your own words and letting them sink in. Then read them every morning and every evening and whenever you sense that you are sliding into a blue mood. You may want to make photocopies to carry with you. If you are an auditory person, you can make a tape recording of them with music you enjoy playing in the background. If you respond well to visual cues, you can purchase a small photograph album, fill it with photos or pictures clipped from magazines, and use your affirmations as captions. In whatever mode you choose, however, regularly rereading your new ideas is essential. Remember that you are trying to break a negative thinking habit you have had for years. It will take a great deal of practice to do that. It is also helpful to add to your list of positive statements as often as possible, with your goal being to accumulate as many uplifting ideas as you once had depressing ones.

JUMPING TO CONCLUSIONS OR OVERGENERALIZING

Some people jump to conclusions, make decisions, or spring into action based on one or two facts (or, more frequently, one or more inaccurate assumptions) that do not tell the whole story. As we have seen, Susan did this twice. First she leaped from feeling that the sergeant's exam was biased to believing that the entire police force was, and then she jumped to the conclusion that because she was a woman, she did not stand a chance of succeeding in the police department.

We also saw Joel do it. He proceeded rapidly from the fact that he had not completed his tax return to the perception that his entire life was out of control.

Matthew did it, too, with an added twist: mind reading. A while back, Matthew and his friend Jerry teamed up to teach a money management course at the local YMCA. The course had been Jerry's idea, one he thought might get Matthew out of his rut. Matthew hated to admit it, but it was working.

Then one evening Jerry phoned to inform Matthew that they would have to cancel the following week's class because he would be out of town. That was fine with him, Matthew told Jerry, but after he hung up, the conversation began to bother him. He wondered why Jerry decided to cancel without consulting him. "Doesn't *my* opinion count for anything? And what makes Jerry think I couldn't handle the class alone? I know every bit as much about money management as he does. Who died and left him in charge?" Matthew could not stop thinking about what he had decided was shabby treatment and an obvious putdown from Jerry. The more he thought, the angrier he got.

After two days of brooding, Matthew finally called Jerry and "blasted him with both barrels." Jerry was shocked. His actual intentions did not even vaguely resemble those that Matthew was attributing to him. He canceled the class because he did not want Matthew to be overcome with the responsibility for it. Thus Matthew had made himself miserable over motives that had never crossed Jerry's mind.

The conclusions you reach will not always be as far off the mark as Matthew's. For instance, Beverly's conclusion that her daughters took advantage of her could be supported by plenty of hard evidence, yet it was still unproductive. It not only made Beverly miserable but also implied that being taken advantage of was a fact of life.

OTHER ALTERNATIVES

Perhaps the most self-defeating aspect of jumping to conclusions is the finality. As the word *conclusion* implies, you have reached the end of the line, arrived at your mental destination. You have made a final decision and are apt to stay with it, ignoring any evidence that contradicts your conclusion (no matter how depressing that conclusion may be). Since it is quite difficult to change your thinking once your mind is made up, your best bet for correcting this cognitive glitch is to break the habit that leads to it. Instead of latching on to the first idea that pops into your mind and running with it, stop to consider other alternatives. Adopt the rule of three.

Before piling on more unproductive thoughts or springing into action, come up with three possible explanations for what is happening or the way you are feeling: the conclusion you were about to jump to *plus* two more. To reduce the possibility that your alternatives will be equally or more defeating than your original premise, make sure neither of the two has anything to do with your inherent inadequacies, contains the words *always, never,* or *nothing ever,* and is not an inaccurate *if/then* statement.

For example, let's say a salesclerk treats you rudely and your typical unproductive conclusion would be: "It figures. No one ever treats me with respect." Two alternative explanations would be: (1) The salesclerk is having a rotten day and taking it out on her customers, and (2) the salesclerk just doesn't treat others as respectfully as you do. Notice that I did not say that the salesclerk *should* treat people more respectfully. That would be another trap. As it is worded, alternative number two could be a reason to pat yourself on the back. You treat people respectfully and can feel proud of that. To derive maximum benefits from the rule of three, try to make at least one alternative have that same sort of positive potential.

In most upsetting situations you cannot prove beyond a shadow of a doubt that any of your three alternatives actually explains what is happening, and therein lies the beauty of the rule of three. You can *choose* to accept and act on the least distressing explanation instead of getting stuck with your usual one (which is invariably the least accurate and the most depressing of the three).

Now give it a try. In your notebook, write what you would typically think plus two alternative explanations for the following situations:

1. You wake up from a nap and find a note from your roommates (with whom you had planned to spend the evening) saying: Didn't want to disturb you so we went out for pizza without you. Will call later so you can meet us at the movies.
2. Two weeks after you submitted a report, your supervisor still has not said anything to you about it.

3. Your spouse has worked late three nights in a row and on the fourth night rejects your sexual overtures.

4. You've had a recent experience that upset you.

DISPROVING YOUR OVERGENERALIZATIONS

If you tend to overgeneralize, you may find it helpful to take on the role of your own defense attorney and come up with concrete evidence to disprove the "charges" you have filed against yourself. You can use any kind of proof you need to defend yourself in front of the toughest judge and jury of them all: yourself. The only thing you cannot do is switch your plea to guilty.

1. File your blanket indictment. At the top of a page in your notebook, write an overgeneralization that is making you miserable, such as "I never accomplish anything," "Nothing good ever happens to me," "No matter how hard I try, I always fail."

2. Gather the evidence you need to defend yourself against the charges. Delve as far back into your memory as you wish and come up with as many specific "facts" as possible to disprove your generalization. Write down instances in which you actually did what you claim never to do. Did you graduate from high school or college? interview for jobs? get them? earn a paycheck? raise children? live outside your parents' home? Then you have accomplished something. Did you try to get out of bed this morning and do it? Then you succeeded. Look for more dramatic evidence too. In your blue frame of mind you have probably forgotten things like getting pay raises or being praised for your volunteer work or having a wonderful time at last year's company picnic. Try going through old photo albums and boxes of memorabilia to help jog your memory.

3. Write a summation to the jury. Being as passionate as possible, wrap up the case for the defense. Convince the judge and jury that your overgeneralization was a distortion of reality, that *always, never,* and *nothing ever* just do not apply. By doing this you not only refute an unproductive point of view but also create a series of accurate, positive thoughts that you can add to your list of affirmations.

NEGATIVE PREDICTIONS

"No matter how hard I try, my boss will never be satisfied with my work."

"It's no use. If I tell my spouse how I feel, we'll only end up in an argument."

"I just know I'm going to say something stupid and embarrass myself."

"I can't do that. I don't have what it takes."

These are just a few examples of the final type of unproductive thinking that often plagues DD sufferers. When you anticipate or predict the future you may:

- *Expect the worst.* Whether you are about to interview for a job, give a speech, go to a party, or ask a friend to do you a favor, you conjure up worst-case scenarios, imagining everything that could possibly go wrong and often dwelling on the most anxiety-provoking item on your list. Joel did this whenever he thought about approaching attractive women at social gatherings. They would turn away from him as if he were invisible, he thought. Judy did this before her co-worker's birthday party, picturing herself "standing alone in the corner like some stupid wallflower."
- *Expect the impossible.* The flip side of expecting the worst, conjuring up best possible fantasies also takes an emotional toll on you. Imagining that your new job will be absolutely perfect, assuming that you and your lover will never disagree, expecting your children to be well behaved and appreciative of everything you do for them sets you up for disappointment. Reality rarely lives up to your grandiose ideals, and you feel cheated. Best-case scenarios sometimes stir up as much anxiety as their negative counterparts. For instance, while Joel was having a drink and mustering up the courage to approach an attractive woman, he would fantasize about how terrific it would be if she was "the real thing," the woman who was his perfect match. He visualized their future together and, by the time he finished his drink, had them married and living in suburbia with their two adorable kids. Suddenly the prospect of being rejected by this woman was much more frightening. After all, she wasn't a stranger anymore but his future wife and the mother of his children.
- *Tell yourself that you "can't."* Instead of tackling a task and doing it to the best of your ability, you use your time and energy to tell yourself why you are incapable of tackling it. This line of thinking frequently follows a "should" (I should be able to get my paperwork done on time, but I can't get organized); a comparison (other people enjoy these parties, but I can't think of anything interesting to say

to anybody); or a run-through of the long list of things you feel obligated to do. Naturally, your "I can't"s reinforce your sense of inadequacy and powerlessness. They also leave you feeling overwhelmed and worried that your entire life might be getting out of control.

All three forms of anticipating and predicting the future stir up a maelstrom of unsettling emotions and all too often become self-fulfilling prophecies. For instance, Joel believed his prediction that attractive women would reject him and therefore did not approach them. He could not get what he wanted and went home believing he never would. Similarly, Judy's mind was often so preoccupied with worries about what to say to people that she barely said anything at all. The resulting one-way conversations made the other people uncomfortable, and they eventually drifted away, leaving Judy to think, "See, I really am dull and boring." Whatever it may be, the dreaded result comes to pass as predicted. You get to be right but certainly not happy.

Likewise, anything you are convinced you cannot do, you generally do not attempt or you leave half-finished because you cannot do it as well as you wish you could. Your pattern of not doing leads to getting nothing done, reinforcing your negative opinion of yourself and keeping you down in the dumps.

"Looking at the Whole Spectrum" Exercise. Like jumping to conclusions, when you anticipate or predict the future you grab on to one idea and run with it. Usually settling upon the prophesized outcome you fear most, you assume that your forecast will come true and act accordingly—more often than not, attempting to avoid the situation that might produce the disaster you have envisioned. As mentioned earlier, avoidance, especially when undertaken without considering alternatives, is invariably self-defeating. It prevents you from discovering that outcomes other than the ones you fear frequently occur and that even if what you predicted comes to pass, it is rarely, if ever, as terrible as you imagined it would be. What is more, you miss out on opportunities to handle stressful situations, if not perfectly, at least adequately, which would counteract all those self-defeating ideas about being a hopeless failure or a powerless victim. To overcome this debilitating obstacle of beating the blues, you must learn to look at the whole spectrum of possible outcomes, from the best to the worst, but most important, everything in between. The following exercise will help you visualize this range:

1. Open your notebook to a clean page. At the top of it, write down an upcoming event that is creating anxiety or dread. If you cannot think of a specific event, use a situation that typically prompts you to anticipate or predict the future.
2. Divide the rest of the page into three sections, labeling the top third Worst Cases, the bottom third Best Cases, and the middle Everything Else.
3. Write down your catastrophic predictions in the Worst Cases section of the page. Ask yourself what could possibly go wrong and come up with some scenarios for the event in question. Feel free to give vent to your most ghastly fantasies.
4. Write your perfect fantasies in the Best Cases section. Ask yourself what the best possible outcome would be. If you could write the perfect script for the upcoming event, what would it say?
5. Fill in the middle ground. Include less than optimal results that are not as catastrophic as your worst-case scenarios, positive outcomes that are realistic rather than fantasies, and neutral occurrences that would represent a respectable showing although not necessarily anything spectacular.
6. Finally, rate the odds for each outcome. Perhaps you found yourself chuckling at some of your own ideas. When looked at realistically, both your best- and worst-case scenarios can be amusing. Chances are that nothing you have written down thus far will ever come to pass. Real outcomes of real situations tend to fall between the two extremes to which you have been devoting so much of your time and energy.

   Which of your outcomes are long shots (LS), so unlikely to occur that no experienced gambler would bet on them? Which have even odds (EO), a 50–50 chance of coming to pass? Which seem to be sure things (ST), the results you are most likely to encounter? Mark each scenario with the initials that describe them.

To give you an idea of what to expect from this strategy, here is a page from Joel's notebook:

Upcoming Event: Dinner meeting with Linda (a woman Joel met after he began working as a volunteer on a congressman's reelection campaign. She is the campaign manager and he finds her attractive.)

Worst Cases

1. I bring flowers to let her know I'm interested in more than a working relationship. She brings along her live-in boyfriend. (LS. She might have a boyfriend, but she wouldn't bring him along.)
2. I drop silverware, spill the wine, drool, and inadvertently make a snide comment about her favorite writer. She makes an excuse to leave before dessert. (LS)
3. She tells me I'm a detriment to the congressman's campaign and suggests that I should stay behind the scenes, perhaps stuffing envelopes. (LS)

Everything Else

1. I don't do anything to embarrass myself; Linda and I have a good time. (EO)
2. I figure out she already has a boyfriend and feel disappointed. (EO)
3. She doesn't have a boyfriend. I ask her out, she says no, I feel rejected and embarrassed. (EO)
4. She doesn't have a boyfriend. I ask her out, she says yes, I feel great. (EO)
5. I'm still not sure if she is interested in me socially, but I suggest that she book my jazz group for a campaign fund-raiser and invite her to come hear us play. She does and we get to know each other better. (EO)
6. I continue to work on the congressman's campaign, take on more responsibility (feeling good about it). I also make an effort to get to know Linda better and if all goes well, ask her out. (ST)

Best Cases

1. The congressman saw the position paper I wrote and asked Linda to offer me a full-time job with a six-figure salary. (LS)
2. Linda seduces me. (LS)
3. I seduce Linda. (EO, but I probably won't have the nerve.)
4. I get into politics, marry Linda, and with her by my side eventually become governor. (LS)

As Joel did, you are apt to discover that the outcomes most likely to come to pass (EOs and STs) rarely involve the horrific consequences you have been envisioning. What actually happens may not elate you, but it will not devastate you either. With that knowledge you may be able to move forward in a more relaxed and confident manner. If there is still even the slightest hint of potential discomfort attached to the event, however, you may remain paralyzed. This generally means that you are still blowing at least one possible consequence out of proportion and need to do a quick reality check.

The problem with negative predictions goes beyond the prediction itself and often lies in the notion that should your fear be realized, it would be catastrophic. Even after you expand your view of the potential outcomes, this feeling that the event will bring about consequences that cause *permanent* and *irreversible* damage to you or your relationships may persist. In reality such catastrophes are almost never the case, but you need not take my word for it. The next time you anticipate disaster, ask yourself if anything that might happen will literally kill you, truly ruin your career and all of your plans for the future, prompt your spouse to divorce you or your family to disown you, or still be causing you pain a year from now. If your answer is no (and 99.9 percent of the time it will be), then it is safe to move forward. It is also more beneficial than staying where you are—stuck on the blue mood merry-go-round.

7

Behavioral Switches: Change What You Do, and It Will Change How You Feel

Although Andrea did plenty of work on her unproductive thinking, action proved to be the key for her to overcome DD. "My first real breakthrough came when I cleaned my bedroom closet," she said. "I know that may sound weird, but it was the first time in years that I started, stayed with, and finished anything. And it was the first time in years that I actually felt good about myself. I could pat myself on the back and say, 'See, you thought you couldn't do it, but you did. You persevered.' " And that got Andrea thinking that she could do other things as well, such as refinishing the wall unit that had been standing in the middle of her living room for five months, unpacking the boxes that had been stacked in her bedroom for five years, painting the walls of her apartment, paving her way back into the fashion industry by repairing garments she bought at flea markets and selling them on consignment at a vintage clothing store. The more Andrea did, the less inadequate and powerless she felt. In fact, she was well on her way to beating the blues.

"I finally figured out that doing nothing was getting me down," Andrea explained. Although you may not have done anything about it yet, you have probably figured that out too. Perhaps you knew it . . .

> . . . when tax time rolled around and you got angry at yourself because, despite your promise to be more organized, your receipts were scattered throughout the house.
> . . . when you found the half-finished afghan in the hall closet, the one you had been crocheting as a birthday gift for your favorite aunt.
> . . . when you woke up three hours later after lying down to take a thirty-minute nap and found your husband and children eating bologna sandwiches for dinner.

At these moments it was easy to see that what you did or did not do brought on your blue mood. Your actions have the same effect over the long haul. Just as your unproductive thinking influences your feelings and actions, your actions influence your thoughts and feelings, sustaining your chronic case of the blues. Behavior therapists have known this for years. They have witnessed depressed individuals acting in ways that deprive them of positive rewards and bring about negative consequences, ones that make them feel even more depressed.

THE CYCLE OF SELF-DEFEAT
On a recent Sunday afternoon, Joel, wearing the same moth-eaten sweatsuit he had slept in the night before, lounged in a comfortable chair, and used his remote-control device to keep track of three football games being televised at once. His apartment was a mess: The Sunday paper was strewn all over the sofa, take-out food cartons littered the coffee table, soiled clothing was draped over furniture or piled in heaps

on the floor. Glancing around at these dismal surroundings, Joel briefly entertained the notion of doing some cleaning but immediately talked himself out of it. "It's not like I'll be bringing a date home tonight," he told himself, "so why bother?"

Finally, as the day drew to a close, Joel decided to do his laundry. Barefoot, with his teeth unbrushed, his hair uncombed, and corn chip crumbs clinging to his sweatshirt, he trudged down to the laundry room. There, reading a magazine while her clothes were drying, was the attractive young woman from down the hall whom Joel had been dying to meet. Suddenly Joel was painfully aware of his sloppy appearance. He hurriedly shoved his clothes into the washer, nodded a curt hello, and left.

"I took the world's fastest shower," Joel explained, "I got dressed, combed my hair, even put on after-shave and returned to the laundry room." But his lovely neighbor was gone. Bitterly disappointed and disgusted with himself, Joel transferred his clothes to the dryer and for the umpteenth time told himself, "I'm such a loser. Nothing I do turns out right. I haven't been in the right place at the right time since the day I was born. So why should I even bother trying anymore?"

Joel had defeated himself, and his self-defeating behavior was self-perpetuating. By not bothering to take certain actions, he suffered consequences that convinced him not to "bother" in the future—virtually guaranteeing that he would go on doing (or not doing) the very same things that were undermining him.

Of course, Joel might argue that his lethargy, lack of interest in his appearance, and "why bother?" attitude were symptoms of his mood disorder, that they were the typical, unavoidable side effects of a chronic case of the blues. He would be right. Over time, however, they had become more than that. By surrendering to his symptoms and accepting them as facts that he was powerless to alter, Joel had unwittingly made it possible for the behavior caused by his depression to depress him further. Although you never intended to, if you have been blue for an extended period of time, you may have done that too.

You have gotten caught in a failure cycle, setting unattainable goals for yourself and then talking yourself out of taking action because you don't stand a chance of succeeding. You may procrastinate or start projects but never finish them because you cannot measure up to your own perfectionistic standards. Or you may make lengthy "to do" lists and become so discouraged by the number of tasks awaiting your attention that you do not get around to accomplishing any of them. The end result of this sort of behavior is the pervasive sense of inadequacy and hopelessness that prevents your blues from going away.

Routine tasks constantly get away from you. Disorganized and lacking the energy or concentration to start or stay with most activities, everyday demands go unmet, daily chores go undone, and things pile up until you feel completely overwhelmed. Like a perverse Greek chorus, those neglected tasks taunt you, reminding you that a better person, a more competent one would have gotten to them by now. But still you do not get to them and begin to feel as if your entire life is out of control. You feel powerless and, of course, depressed.

Opting for whatever requires the least amount of energy, you devote the bare minimum of your time to productive or truly enjoyable activities. Your "activity diet" lacks nourishing experiences. You derive little satisfaction from your work, have few leisure activities that stimulate your interest, and put yourself under house arrest so that you have little or no social contact with other people. As a result, you rarely get a chance to experience pleasure or a positive sense of accomplishment and self-worth. On the other hand, you have ample opportunities to sit around feeling sorry for yourself and examining under a microscope everything that is wrong with you or missing from your life.

If you want results that are different from the ones I have just described, then you are going to have to behave differently. You are going to have to manage your time, take steps to relieve your energy-draining physical symptoms, get organized, be more active in general, and increase pleasurable activities in particular.

MANAGING YOUR TIME

If I asked you to, I am sure you could think of at least a dozen things you have been meaning to do. Some are dull but necessary tasks that you would like to cross off your "to do" list. Others, such as going on a diet, getting out to meet new people, or updating your résumé and looking for a new job, are steps you could take to solve problems that are depressing you. Still others are activities that could soothe or amuse you, adding some much needed comfort or pleasure to your life. If I pressed you,

you would also admit that you would feel better if you did those things, not necessarily on top of the world but at least competent, in control, productive, and proud of yourself. Yet knowing this is rarely enough to counteract the feeling that you are already overwhelmed by the demands of daily living and stretched to the limit. If you are like most DD sufferers, you sincerely believe that you do not have the time to do what you need to do to feel better.

This barrier to behaving differently is generally a matter of not using your time effectively rather than not having the time to use. To find out if that is true for you, try conducting a time study.

1. Make some copies of the Personal Activities Chart (table 2) . It is designed to help you clarify what you do during the day and how much time you spend doing it.
2. Keep account of your time for one week, stopping at intervals during the day (early morning, mid-morning, noon, midafternoon, evening, and bedtime) to chronicle exactly how you used your time since the previous notation. In the Type column, use the letter *O* (for obligation) to denote activities you *had* to do, the letter *C* for those things you freely *chose* to do, and the letter *A* (for automatic) for anything you did without knowing or paying attention to what you were doing or why. Rate these as positive (+), neutral (0), or negative (−) experiences (see page 126).

Here is Ralph's account of one morning period:

In bed, reviewing things I had to do that day: 20 min. (A)
Running late, rushed through bathroom routine: 10 min. (O)
Got dressed (couldn't decide what tie to wear, got lost in thought while putting on my socks): 30 min. (O, A)
Drove to work (skipped breakfast): 15 min. (O)
Stayed in break room talking (C), drinking coffee (C), eating doughnuts (A): 30 min.
Worked: 15 min. (O)
Listened to colleagues discussing pretty client: 10 min. (A)
Worked: 30 min. (O)
Worried about investments: 10 min. (A)
Borrowed a *Wall Street Journal*, stopped to talk, read the stock pages: 20 min. (C)

TABLE 2
PERSONAL ACTIVITIES CHART

DAY/DATE:					
ACTIVITY	TIME USED	TYPE	(+)	(0)	(−)
Code: A = Automatic C = Chose to do O = Obligation					

3. If you are reluctant to commit yourself to such detailed record-keeping, you can take the following shortcut. It will not provide as much useful data, but it will give you a general picture of how you are using your time. Think of four days during the past month—a representative weekday, a representative weekend day (or day off from work or school), a day that seemed particularly hectic and one when you felt more depressed than usual. Reconstruct in as much detail as possible exactly what you did on that day and how much time you spent on each endeavor. Put it on the chart.

With this method, Andrea's typical weekday looked like this:

Get up, get dressed, and so forth: 1 hour (O)
Breakfast in front of the TV: 30 min. (A)
Travel to work: 20 min. (O)
Work: 8 hours (O)
Travel from work: 20 min. (O)
Stop to buy fast food and magazine: (C)
Eat and read magazine: 1 hour (C)
Make phone calls: 30 min. (C)
Watch TV and snack: 3 hours (A)
Sleep: 9 hours (C, O, A?)

These two examples show the connection between the blues and behavior. In a three-hour time span, Ralph spent an hour—one-third of his time—brooding, worrying, and thinking. Since this left him playing catchup for the remaining two-thirds of his time, it is no wonder that he constantly felt overwhelmed. And Andrea spent eight hours at a job she hated, nine hours sleeping, and three and a half hours watching TV—which she admits she does not particularly enjoy. If you include forty minutes of commuting on congested freeways that frighten Andrea, you get a daily routine that might depress even the cheeriest optimist. Looking closely at your own Activities Chart, you will probably find similar connections as well as other behavioral sources of your blues. You will also begin to see some things you can minimize in order to have time for things that will help you feel better.

GETTING ORGANIZED

Although by eliminating nonessential, nonnourishing, and depressing activities, anyone with a chronic case of the blues can make room on his or her schedule for productivity and pleasure, this rearranging and changing of priorities is much easier to achieve when you employ the following time management techniques, which will also help you feel less harried and overwhelmed in general.

1. **Plan:** Write down what you have to do each day. This shortens the time spent mentally reviewing your obligations. It also reduces anxiety over possibly forgetting an important task and alerts you to the possibility that your expectations for one day are not realistic.

2. **Prioritize:** Imagine the chaos that would result in a hospital emergency room if all the patients were assumed to be equally in need of immediate attention. Not only would the staff be in a state of panic, but while they were hurrying to care for those with minor problems, the patients with more serious difficulties would expire. The idea of equal importance does not make sense in an emergency room, and it does not make sense in your life either. Instead of treating all your responsibilities as if they were urgent and equal to one another, prioritize the items on your "to do" list. Each time you have to make a decision about how to use your time, let your preset priorities be your guide.

3. **Delegate:** Identify any items on your daily schedule or "to do" list that other people could do or help you do. Give up the unproductive notion that to have something done right you must do it yourself or that requesting assistance is a sign of weakness. Go ahead and ask for the help you need. You can save additional time by allowing the people whose help you've requested do as you've asked without hovering over them, checking up on them, or going back to improve upon the job when it is finished.

4. **Stop assuming unwanted responsibility, especially other people's:** If your co-workers want to take up a collection and send flowers to your recuperating supervisor, you do not have to be the one to do it. If your daughters want to go to the mall, you do not have to drive them both ways or at all. If your church needs someone to chair a fund-raising drive, you do not have to volunteer for the job. If such nonessential activities are adding more drudgery and no satisfaction to your life, stop doing them. You will take even more pressure off and cut down on feelings of resentment if you also stop doing things for other people that they are perfectly capable of doing themselves or that you do not have to do (picking up your children's dirty socks from the floor, getting your husband's shirts from the laundry, taking a co-worker's calls when he is out of the office, for example).

5. **Combine or condense activities whenever possible:** Pay bills while watching TV, have your son do his homework in the kitchen so that you can help him while you cook dinner. Shop for groceries twice a week instead of three, organize errands so that you do the least amount of driving: These are just a few ways to combine or condense tasks and obligations in order to save time and feel more in control of your life.

6. **Reduce the amount of time you spend "lost in thought":** The tendency to get lost in thought means it will take you longer to complete a task. Mentally drifting off into space is a difficult habit to break, but purchasing a watch with an alarm or an inexpensive kitchen timer may help. If you set the alarm to go off after a specific amount of time or at fifteen-minute intervals, it will interrupt any trances you may have fallen into and get you back on track.

7. **Respect your inner time clock:** You may know from experience that you are not a morning person or that you seem to run out of steam at four in the afternoon and get a second wind by five-thirty or six. If you have been using the self-monitoring strategy found in chapter four, you have an even clearer idea of when your energy level rises and falls. You can use this self-knowledge to your advantage and get more done in less time if you schedule complex or tiring tasks for the times when you have the most energy.

If you would like to learn more or develop more time-management proficiency, consult the resources listed in the bibliography under Behavior Therapy.

With these time-management techniques in mind, you can return to your Personal Activities Chart and begin making room for pleasure and productivity by identifying the tasks or activities that you can eliminate entirely, reduce, combine, or do in less time. Manipulate the items on your chart until you have located a minimum of three hours per week to be used for the sole purpose of feeling better.

ELIMINATING YOUR ENERGY-DRAINING CAUSES

Of course, time is not the only obstacle to behaving in a way different from the past. Both before and after finding time to feel better, most DD sufferers ask: "Where am I supposed to find the energy to do these things?" Lethargy is a symptom of your mood disorder, so claiming to be low on energy is more than an excuse not to change your behavior; you really are physically tired and emotionally drained. It is more difficult to take actions that people without DD take in stride. In fact, it is unreasonable to expect yourself to be efficient and enthusiastic when you are down in the dumps. It is equally unreasonable, however, to put yourself on the disabled list and wait for your blues to go away. Sitting on the sidelines watching the game of life being played by everyone but you only makes you more depressed, further draining your energy rather than replenishing it. Change the pattern by committing yourself to one modest activity—and see it through. This seemingly simple act of overcoming inertia will produce results: The act of moving away from an established pattern toward a less comfortable but more challenging state of being will pay off in an almost immediate sense of increased self-worth.

Adequate Sleep. In order to be active, you need an adequate amount of sleep—neither too little nor too much. Sleeping too little robs you of energy and makes you cranky, less able to cope, and of course more exhausted. If you have a difficult time falling asleep, consider the following suggestions: Try to make the last hours of the day especially relaxing. Listen to your favorite music, read, or take a warm bath. Make your bedroom as relaxing and comfortable as possible. Keep the temperature constant. Wear loose, nonconstricting night clothes. Keep a dim nightlight burning and, if you find it soothing, a radio playing softly.

Rather than lying in the dark telling yourself how terrible you are going to feel tomorrow if you don't fall asleep soon, turn on a light and read something that is not stimulating (the encyclopedia or an almanac, for example) or do a crossword puzzle. Listen to a relaxation tape. Avoid sleeping pills (which can make matters worse, as I will explain later), arguments, soul-searching discussions, and heavy meals before bedtime.

A Tranquil and Relaxing Environment. If your blue moods are accompanied by restlessness and agitation, you will be plagued periodically with heart palpitations, dizziness, thoughts racing through your mind, muscle tension, and other symptoms of anxiety, and you will be supersensitive to your surroundings. Since it is best to avoid anxiety-provoking stimuli, try to make your environment more tranquil: Turn off or lower the radio or television volume, shut windows to muffle the sound of traffic, and stay away from agitating music. If possible, adjust the lighting so that it produces a warm glow rather than a blinding glare.

In addition, learn how to relax—not just putting your feet up and doing nothing but using specific techniques that produce noticeable physical sensations of relaxation and a calm, serene mental state to go with them. Relaxation training is suggested by most mental health professionals and many self-help books as a standard procedure for reducing anxiety and increasing emotional and physical well-being. You can find a technique that suits you in a book on stress management, by purchasing audio tapes that guide you through the entire process, or by trying biofeedback or flotation tanks, which are available in most major cities.

Exercise. Although most DD sufferers shudder at the thought of it, physical activity in general and regular exercise in particular are extremely effective antidepressants as well as proven methods for increasing your energy level. They distract you from your negative mood and take your mind off problems and blue feelings. Additionally, because they reduce both muscle and psychological tension, exercise and other physical activities often promote more restful, refreshing sleep. If you exercise for at least twenty minutes a day, four or five days a week, you will reap all of these benefits.

The best way to start is to become slightly more active, perhaps parking your car farther from your destination and walking, or taking the stairs instead of an elevator or the escalator. Look into different exercise options, try a few, and select one that suits you. If you choose something you enjoy, more likely you will stay with it. If you find a friend to share this exercise activity, you will have additional motivation and the added bonus of reducing your sense of social isolation.

Medications. Consult your physician to see if you are taking any medications that might cause depression or lethargy. Do not overlook those that were prescribed or recommended to help you sleep or relax. Many sleeping pills interrupt or eliminate the stage of sleep called rapid eye movement (REM), leaving you irritable or fatigued and limiting their value. Minor tranquilizers like Valium or Librium may relax you, but they are depressants and can exacerbate your blue mood. If you suspect that any medication is contributing to your blues, ask your doctor about alternatives.

In addition to relieving the uncomfortable physical symptoms of DD and supplying you with enough energy to pursue productive and pleasurable activities, the measures just described can put the law of inertia to work for you. Since you have been doing very little for quite some time, you are already familiar with the down side of this phenomenon—that things at rest tend to remain at rest. By taking action in the above areas, you get to experience the up side—that things in motion tend to remain in motion. Once you get moving you will find it easier to keep moving, to keep doing whatever it takes to feel better.

SETTING GOALS AND ACHIEVING THEM

While in the throes of your chronic case of the blues, you lost touch with the process of doing. You stopped seeing yourself as a person who sets out to do something, stays with it, and gets it done. That is the way you may have operated once, but now it seems as if you are paralyzed by even the simplest tasks. When you think about the months and years you have been depressed, you are apt to see a vast wasteland littered with broken promises, untended friendships, unfinished projects, and unattained goals. Consequently, the mere thought of returning to the things you unintentionally let get away from you may exhaust you. Surveying the road that lies ahead may be even more discouraging. It seems as if you will have far to go before you have a "normal" life again. Just looking at the "big picture" can be completely overwhelming. The best thing to do is *not* to look at the big picture. Instead, focus on one specific, attainable goal at a time and devote your efforts to achieving it. "First things first" is the maxim to keep in mind while trying to become more productive, and only one task (not twenty) can come first.

Andrea's new therapist thought that Andrea needed to accomplish something and suggested that she tackle one of the problem areas she had mentioned in passing: her overstuffed, disorganized bedroom closet.

"What do you mean, clean my closet?" Andrea asked in bewilderment, "That closet's the least of my problems! If I'm going to put my energy into anything, it should be getting my career back on track!" Andrea had just made a mistake that many people with the blues make: She dismissed a task that was within her grasp in order to save her limited physical and emotional resources for something that "really mattered"— the most global and ambitious goal that came to mind.

When asked to define a goal for yourself, you probably do that too. You don't set your sights on anything as mundane as getting the unanswered mail off your desk, learning a relaxation technique, reading a book on how to return to the job market, or organizing a closet. Instead, you "go for the gold": to feel happy, to be more like your outgoing, self-confident brother, to have a good marriage, a fulfilling career, or an exciting social life. There is nothing actually wrong with those goals; they can remain your ultimate destination. You are unlikely to reach that destination, however, if you disregard the steps that take you there.

Changing your behavior in order to feel better is like building a pyramid, and you build it from the bottom up. It is imperative to start by tackling the seemingly insignificant things because they are pieces of the "big picture," parts of the larger problem you want to solve or the loftier goal you want to achieve. But before you take on huge projects or make major life changes, you need a track record of success. You have not accomplished much lately, and you need to prove that you can. Otherwise your fear of failure or your sense of powerlessness and inadequacy will keep you inactive, waiting for your circumstances to improve on their own or for some miraculous change to come over you to make you capable of tackling something new.

SMALL STEPS TO SUCCESS
Follow the steps below to accomplish your tasks:

Step One: Set a specific, attainable goal. By identifying your goal, you make a major leap toward restoring your sense of competency and accomplishment. To be useful and improve your chances to achieve it successfully, the goal must be specific and attainable. Consider the following when determining whether your goal fits that description:

Make sure the task is not too big; if you feel overwhelmed by it, then it needs to be broken down into smaller pieces. For example, Andrea initially chose to fix up her apartment, but when she thought about its condition after five years of neglect, she became disheartened, exhausted, and more depressed. After sitting down and listing everything that "fixing up" her apartment would entail, she chose one item on that list: cleaning her bedroom closet, as her therapist had originally suggested, and made that her goal.

Make sure you fully understand what you want to accomplish. Connie didn't. Her idea of having quality time with her kids was at best a foggy notion. She had to be more specific and describe her goal in terms of concrete, observable behavior. By modifying her goal so that it was to spend at least two hours a week with her kids doing things they like to do, she knew exactly what she would do and how she would know when she had done it. Your goal should also meet these two criteria.

Make sure your goal is right for you today. Because many DD sufferers long for the good old days and assume that feeling better means returning to the way they were before they got the blues, they tend to set goals that might have been attainable at one time but do not fit their present circumstances. For instance, Joel wanted to develop a circle of friends to do things with on the weekends. Although this appeared to be a reasonable goal, Joel later realized that he was trying to re-create the experiences he had during his college days when everyone he knew had approximately the same life-style and being part of a group virtually guaranteed something to do. Joel would probably not find such a homogeneous group and activities were not guaranteed. Since he was setting himself up to be disappointed, he remedied the situation by splitting his goal in two: He would ask fellow teachers, his jazz musician friends, and casual acquaintances to join him in activities, and he would join a group to meet new people. He chose to pursue the latter goal first. Check your goal for timeliness and modify it if necessary.

Make sure the goal is right for you personally. Another trap many DD sufferers fall into is letting other people set their agenda for them: losing ten pounds because your mother wants you to; taking an aerobics class because your friend does; returning to school because your brother thinks you should. If you fall into that trap, you will find it more difficult to adhere to your plans. It is best to freely choose a course of action that you personally want to pursue.

Step Two: Keep it simple. When Andrea decided to clean her bedroom closet, she thought that she should also repaint it, paper the overhead shelf, purchase and install colorful shoe or sweater racks, and perhaps carpet its floor. In aiming to make the end result "perfect," she managed to make the assignment more difficult, more costly, and more time-consuming, all of which Andrea could have turned into an excuse *not* to do what she originally set out to do.

By adding unnecessary extras, you turn a straightforward task into an overwhelming production and then are tempted to abandon it. To prevent this as well as the paralysis that results from thinking, "If I can't do it perfectly, I won't do it at all," write down your objectives—the reasons you want to accomplish this particular task. Keep them simple and aim for what you need rather than what you wish you could obtain based on your "best possible" fantasy.

Andrea came up with three reasonable objectives: to be able to find the clothes she wants to wear without tearing everything apart; to have enough room so that things can hang without getting wrinkled; and to make extra storage space.

Similarly, Connie decided that what she really wanted was to: spend some time with her boys every day; get to know their interests and talents; let them know that they are important to her.

Connie realized that she did not have to stage major and exhausting "happenings" in order to get what she wanted.

By identifying the results you want, you can focus your efforts on only those measures that will achieve them.

Step Three: Make an approach plan. Like a pilot filing a flight plan before takeoff, developing an approach plan enables you to map out the best possible route to your destination and allows you to clarify how you are going to get the job done. This increases your efficiency and decreases the potential for unforeseen obstacles to hamper your progress further down the line.

Establish checkpoints: Break the task at hand into small pieces. Don't worry about the sequence of events but try to envision every little thing the task will entail, then write it all down.

Check the "weather" forecast: Attempt to identify any potential obstacles or problems you might encounter. Put your tendency to anticipate disasters and resist change to work for you. Identify the measures you can employ to prevent problems or overcome obstacles. Your solutions are likely to include some of the time-management or symptom relief strategies discussed earlier, as well as the ways to get off the blue mood merry-go-round found in chapter four.

Prepare for your "flight": Think about what you need to know or have on hand in order to accomplish your goal. Be as specific as possible and include how or where you will obtain these prerequisites. This step may be as simple as obtaining boxes and labels for storing things when you clean out the attic to marking the contents of each box. Or you may need to do background research—learning about nutrition, for example, or coming up with a list of places where you could meet new people; you may have to learn a new skill, take an assertiveness training course, or enroll in a money management class. Add your preparation steps to your list.

Plan to "refuel": Identify some rewards you can build into your plan as added incentives to keep working toward your goal. Although accomplishing the goal will be a reward in itself, it is beneficial to include a few positive reinforcers along the way. You might want to buy yourself small presents, read a magazine, take a bubble bath, get a massage, or go out to a nice restaurant for dinner after accomplishing steps toward your goal. You should verbally praise yourself every step of the way and definitely reward yourself when the goal is accomplished. Add your rewards to the list.

Step Four: Schedule your steps. Look over your approach plan and select what you will do first. Determine how much time it will take, then decide exactly when you will begin. If it will take a number of days or weeks to complete, decide how long you intend to spend on it each day. On your calendar, pencil the task into your schedule. Repeat this process for the second, third, fourth, and fifth tasks. To avoid overwhelming and overburdening yourself and to be able to see progress, try not to schedule more than five tasks.

Step Five: Do what you have planned. One at a time, perform each task and adhere to your schedule. Do not postpone a task without a very good reason—being tired or down in the dumps does *not* qualify as a good reason. If you find that you cannot spend as much time as you scheduled, make the most of the time you can devote to the task. Try not to waste your allotted time fretting over what needs to be done, just do it.

Your habits of procrastinating, leaving things half-finished, or giving up before you begin are not easy to break. Sometimes you will be tempted to talk yourself out of doing what you had planned. Sometimes you will find yourself sitting around moping and brooding as you did in the past. When this happens, try *the five-minute plan:* Make a pact with yourself to devote just five minutes to the task you had scheduled (or any other productive activity). Tell yourself that after five minutes you can, if you want to, go back to doing nothing and thinking about how miserable you are. Generally, before the five minutes are up, you will find yourself willing and able to continue. If on a rare occasion you don't, give yourself a break. Nobody's perfect.

As you attend to each task on your list, check it off. When you have completed all five steps on your calendar, schedule five more. This process allows you to always know where you stand. It also reminds you that you are making progress. You are moving forward, accomplishing things, doing what you thought you would never be able to do. Give yourself a well-deserved pat on the back and keep moving. You will discover that each accomplishment adds to your sense of competence and self-worth. The more you do, the better you will feel, and before you know it, your blue mood will begin to lift.

Of course, there is more to life and overcoming DD than being productive. There is also pleasure, something seldom experienced by people with chronic cases of the blues.

PLEASURABLE ACTIVITIES

In the small New Jersey law firm where Ralph worked, the attorneys had lunch together every Monday, a tradition begun long before Ralph arrived and one he usually enjoyed. Those lunches, with their freewheeling discussions of legal issues and their hilarious roasting of the firm's more eccentric clients, were often just what Ralph needed to lift his spirits after a weekend spent brooding over the depressing aspects of his life. One Monday, Ralph—who had been down in the dumps for the past three years—needed cheering up more than ever but chose not to go to lunch with his colleagues.

"I didn't feel like listening to them talk about the terrific weekends they'd had," said Ralph. "Besides, my paperwork was so backed up that I figured I could use the peaceful hour to catch up on some of it." Although he fully intended to spend that hour productively, ten minutes after his colleagues left, Ralph began feeling resentful. If they weren't so noisy and distracting when they were around, he wouldn't have gotten behind on his paperwork in the first place, he told himself. He stared at the case notes scribbled on his yellow legal pad, but they remained incomprehensible.

He thought that his co-workers were probably as backed up as he was but they weren't responsible enough to care. He started to draft a letter but could not remember one of the points he had planned to make. He decided he must be the most responsible person in the office, but then wondered why he was punishing himself by skipping lunch. Ralph decided that he deserved a break and that he was "darn well going to take one." Forty minutes after the other attorneys departed, Ralph left the office to eat lunch alone, imagining and feeling miserable about the stimulating conversation he had missed by not lunching with his colleagues. The service at the restaurant was slow, the traffic on the way back to the office was horrendous, and he returned an hour after everyone else. When Ralph rushed in, he was late for an important meeting with the firm's senior partner and one of its most prestigious clients. Still behind on his paperwork, Ralph felt more depressed than ever and also looked irresponsible.

If Ralph had let his best interests rather than his blue mood dictate his actions, he would not have stayed mired in his own resentment, eaten a miserable lunch alone, gotten in trouble with two people whose respect and approval he wanted, or become more depressed. By forsaking something he might have enjoyed, he robbed himself of a plus (something that would lift his spirits) and added three minuses (things that depressed him) to his Personal Activities Chart. What is more, because Ralph, like most DD sufferers, regularly chose not to pursue pleasurable activities, his life had little joy or satisfaction in it.

Take Your Pleasure Pulse. Like Ralph, depressed individuals frequently skip potentially pleasurable activities, choosing instead to devote their time to things they think they *should* do. They decide that they must get their life in order before allowing themselves to have fun, or they conclude that because they are in a foul mood, they would not enjoy themselves anyway. In addition, DD sufferers often derive little pleasure or satisfaction from activities they enjoyed before they came down with their chronic case of the blues. This all adds up to a "balance sheet" of pluses and minuses that is heavily weighted on the minus side. Is yours?

Look at your Personal Activities Chart. You can use the last three columns to find out how well or how poorly you are balancing life's pluses and minuses. For each activity you listed, check:

- *the plus* (+) *column* for activities that brought you pleasure, the ones that soothed, amused, relaxed, or pleased you, made you smile or laugh or in any way enhanced your sense of self-worth.
- *the minus* (−) *column* for activities that had a negative impact on you, that exhausted, agitated, frustrated, angered, displeased, or depressed you or in any way diminished your sense of self-worth.
- *the zero* (0) *column* for activities that were neutral, the ones that had no emotional impact on you, that had neither negative nor positive value for you.

Thanks to your chronic blues, most of your daily activities were apt to receive neutral or minus ratings. Sometimes you simply did not do anything from which you could derive pleasure. In other instances the activities might have been enjoyable had you been in a better frame of mind. Go back through your negative and neutrally rated activities and put a star beside the ones you used to enjoy before you got the blues. Also put a star beside those you think you could enjoy if you no longer had the blues.

People with chronic cases of the blues rarely find a day in which most of their activities get plus ratings. If you did, though, it means one of two things: Either your life is not as hopelessly bland, boring, and disheartening as you keep telling yourself or you did something right that day, something that lifted your mood at least temporarily. Since you may want to replicate that behavior in the future, jot down the uplifting activities that seemed to make a difference on that "plus" day.

Now that you know where you stand, you can improve the balance of pluses and minuses in order to derive more satisfaction and experience more pleasure from daily living. Working on your unproductive thinking, self-defeating behavior patterns, and problematic interpersonal relationships will help. As your overall outlook improves, so will your ability to feel good about and enjoy the things you are already doing. You can also take an active role in increasing the joy and fulfillment in your life. You can consciously seek out and engage in additional pleasurable activities.

Make a few copies of the Pleasure Inventory Chart (table 3), and then follow the directions below:

In the wide left-hand column, list your ideas for twenty potentially pleasurable activities. Here are a few ideas to get you started: calling a friend or relative long-distance; renting a comedy for your VCR; taking a bath with all the trimmings: bubbles, soothing music, candlelight, and

TABLE 3
PLEASURE INVENTORY CHART

(1) 20 THINGS YOU MIGHT ENJOY DOING	(2)	(3)	(4)	(5)	(6)	(7)
1)						
2)						
3)						
4)						
5)						
6)						
7)						
8)						
9)						
10)						
11)						
12)						
13)						
14)						
15)						
16)						
17)						
18)						
19)						
20)						

so forth; doing needlepoint, flower arranging, quilting, birdhouse building, or some other craft; reading a "trashy" novel or gossip magazine; trying a new or exotic restaurant for dinner; puttering in the garden.

In addition, try recalling things you used to enjoy doing. It may help to think in terms of three types of pleasure: *the sensual* (baking bread and filling your home with its delightful aroma, listening to music on tape or in concert, taking a drive in the country to view the fall colors, wearing silky lingerie, or anything else that is pleasing to one or more of your five senses); *the interpersonal* (chatting with a friend, going for a walk with your spouse, making mudpies with your children, flirting, and anything else that allows you to enjoy the pleasure of another person's company); *activities that involve mastery* (arts, crafts, stamp collecting, rock climbing, and other hobbies, tinkering with your car or your personal computer, learning to type, play tennis, or speak a foreign language, and anything else that involves mastering a new skill or increasing your proficiency in some area).

After your list has twenty items on it, find out more about the things you like to do:

1. A well-balanced activity diet includes both time alone and time spent in the presence of other people. In the first narrow column write the letter *A* beside activities that you would prefer to do by yourself or that would get you "away from it all." Write an *S* beside each activity that provides an opportunity to socialize.
2. Most DD sufferers are sorely lacking activities that calm their nerves and enable them to relax. Write the letter *R* in the second narrow column to indicate which of your potentially pleasurable activities would provide relaxation.
3. As someone with a chronic case of the blues, you are apt to have few opportunities to benefit from the curative powers of laughter. Denote with an *H* in the third narrow column which of the twenty things you might enjoy doing that could reactivate your sense of humor.
4. Anything that distracts you from your usual worrying and feeling sorry for yourself is a plus. Mark with a *D* in the fourth column those items on your list that fit this description.
5. In the fifth, slightly wider column, write at least one additional benefit you could get from engaging in each activity.
6. In the last column, use the letter *N* to denote any potentially plea-

surable activities that you could begin enjoying immediately and the letter *P* to denote those that require advance planning.

Now that you know what you *can* do and understand the benefits you could obtain by doing those things, it is up to you to do them, to take steps to put more pleasure in your life. A vague intention to have fun one of these days is not sufficient. At least for the time being you need to schedule potentially pleasurable activities, using the Small Steps to Success and actually making appointments to experience pleasure. Write them on your calendar like any other appointment. If you discover that you have only a half hour to spare in a day, break the time into five-minute chunks and create a series of mini-breaks for yourself. And keep those appointments. Putting joy, relaxation, and even a few frivolous moments back into your life is part of what you need to do to overcome DD.

Tuning in to Pleasure. Unfortunately, and as you found out while taking your pleasure pulse, simply engaging in a potentially pleasurable activity does not guarantee that you will derive pleasure from it. You may have gotten out of the habit of feeling pleasure while under the influence of a chronic case of the blues. You become so preoccupied with your blue feelings and unproductive thoughts that you got into the habit of tuning out pleasurable sensations. Here is how to tune in to them again:

1. Pick a short, simple activity—browsing in your favorite bookstore, looking through a seed catalog for flowers to plant in the garden, taking a bubble bath with your favorite music playing in the background—and use it as your testing ground.
2. Before you begin, take thirty seconds to empty your mind. Picture sadness, anxiety, and frustration as blue water being slowly emptied from a laboratory beaker or gray sooty air being blown away by a giant electric fan until only clear, fresh air remains.
3. Imagine that you have just regained use of your senses after a long period of deprivation. In your mind describe everything you see, hear, smell, and touch. Ask yourself questions about what your senses are experiencing and answer them. If your mind starts to wander, bring it back into focus with more questions and answers. If unsettling thoughts intrude, use the thought-stopping technique

found on page 98 and then return your attention to what you are doing.

4. Expand your thinking to include your feelings about what you are experiencing. Put them into words: "The sky is lovely. The flowers smell wonderful. The air is so fresh and clean this morning, and just listen to those birds. Yes, I am enjoying this!" Your thoughts need not be poetic or complex, simply truthful.

5. When you are ready to move on, acknowledge your experience once more. Savor it. Retell it to yourself as you might describe it to a friend whom you hoped to convince to try it too.

6. Repeat this process during the next pleasurable activity you have scheduled, and the ones after that, until you find it easy to tune in to pleasure. Return to this technique whenever you discover yourself "just going through the motions" during an activity you would enjoy if you allowed yourself to.

You now have the basic tools for engaging in behavior that will deactivate the physical switches of your blues merry-go-round: time management, symptom relief, goal setting and achievement, being more productive, and balancing the pluses and minuses in your life. None of these options is perfect, and you will not do any of them perfectly. You may stumble at first and even slip back into your old self-defeating habits from time to time, which is the way change is. As you become accustomed to your new behaviors and experience their rewards, however, they will become new self-enhancing habits, so much a part of your life that you will not always have to go through all the steps and all the planning that has been described. By experimenting and by doing, you will accomplish the goal that has seemed beyond your reach for years: making the blues go away.

8
Interpersonal Switches: Relationship Glitches

On a recent Friday morning Ralph was in the break room eating two stale jelly doughnuts when one of the paralegals entered and gave him what he thought was a disapproving look. "You're right, I'm hopelessly weak-willed and a fool to think I'll ever drop those ten pounds I keep saying I want to lose," he snapped, and stormed past the flabbergasted paralegal, who had not been thinking any such thing.

Ralph felt bad about his outburst and promised himself that he would try harder to control his temper, but only moments after he had stopped berating himself and gotten back to his work, the sound of two male colleagues discussing their weekend plans began to annoy him. "I wish they would keep quiet. How am I supposed to get any work done with them chattering like a couple of school kids?" he grumbled as he got up, angrily stomped across his office, and slammed the door shut. Startled, his colleagues' topic of conversation switched to what a "bear" Ralph had been lately and how everyone at the law firm disappeared when they saw him coming. (Perhaps that was why Ralph had added "getting the cold shoulder" and "a lack of camaraderie at the office" to the list of things that were depressing him.)

Danielle's enthusiasm about her prestigious commission had almost vanished by the time Greg explained the details of their trip to Hawaii— plans that he had made without consulting her. His presumption that she would drop everything to go anywhere with him outraged her. Yet she did not express those feelings. *"That's just the way Greg is,"* Danielle thought, justifying her silence after the fact. *"He's very aggressive about his career. When he wants something, when something is important to him, nothing stands in his way."*

But what about her career? What about her hectic schedule? What about the respect she deserved as an individual with her own wants and needs? "Well, being an artist isn't exactly as important as being a pediatric surgeon," Danielle explained, minimizing the value of her work and in the process devaluing herself. "It's not like I save lives or anything. In fact, it's really sort of frivolous. That's what Greg thinks anyway, and he's probably right." Danielle was no longer angry at Greg. Instead, she was doubting her own worth and her right to the common courtesy of being consulted about matters that concerned her.

Like many chronically depressed individuals, whenever Marcia, the guidance counselor who lived in fear of losing her husband, was left alone, her blue moods worsened. She tried to have people around her at all times, and when she could not, she used the telephone as a lifeline connecting her to the outside world. Consequently, one day when she was home with the flu and feeling exceptionally isolated and vulnerable, her dialing finger was working overtime. Her husband, Jack, was the recipient of most of her calls—a half-dozen of them before noon. By the time the seventh call came through, Jack had had it: "Damn it, Marcia, you have to stop calling here every two minutes," he admonished her and immediately wished he had not.

"Right away she started crying," Jack recalled. "Just sort of whimpering at first and saying how she didn't realize talking to her was such a hardship, how she hated being such a burden to me, how I must really hate her, all that stuff. I tried to explain that I didn't mind talking to her but that I just couldn't talk to her right then. I told her I'd call her back when I could talk, but I don't know if she heard me or not." Sobbing, Marcia swore she would never call Jack at work ever again and hung up.

Having been through similar conversations on countless occasions, Jack tried to shrug this one off, and as he said he would, at his next free moment he returned his wife's call. He got no answer. He tried again an hour later, and there was still no answer. Finally, at four-thirty, he got through.

"Where have you been?" Jack asked. "I've been trying to reach you for hours."

"You have?" Marcia said, sounding truly amazed at Jack's comment. She apologized and explained. "I wanted to get some sleep so I turned off the bell on the phone, and then I forgot to turn it back on again. I had no idea you'd decide to call me after you told me how much you hated talking to me."

"I was ready to tear my hair out," Jack recalled. "She was putting her words in my mouth, but I'd never convince her of that." One thing was certain: The *last* thing Jack wanted was to give Marcia the comfort and reassurance she had originally been seeking. He felt angry and abused, and, as you might expect, this intensified Marcia's fears of losing Jack— and her blue mood.

Relationships can be the source of numerous mood-elevating "pluses" to add to your balance sheet of life experiences. As you can see, Ralph, Danielle, and Marcia did not tap into that potential or obtain those interpersonal pluses. Most DD sufferers do not. Instead, they experience interpersonal friction, anxiety, frustration, disappointment, loneliness, and diminished self-confidence. Indeed, many chronically blue individuals have long, perplexing histories of failed or unfulfilling relationships, and most have a dismal track record when it comes to obtaining even a smidgen of what they want or need from any interpersonal encounter.

If you have a chronic case of the blues, chances are that you relate to people in ways that are not positively reinforcing and that prevent you from obtaining feedback or making emotional connections that would confirm your self-worth and relieve your blue mood. Instead, you reinforce your preconceived notions that other people are insensitive and uncaring or that you are inadequate and unlovable—and, naturally, this perpetuates your chronic case of the blues. If you are like the vast majority of DD sufferers, you do not have the vaguest idea why your interpersonal encounters never seem to work to your advantage or why the most negative assumptions in your blue mood mind-set constantly seem to come true. Your interpersonal difficulties get filed under that catchall heading of things that are hopeless and beyond your control.

But are they really? Or are factors that you *can* alter—runaway emotions, unproductive thinking, and self-defeating behavior—contributing to the problem? Perhaps you are . . .

. . . short on social skills, especially those that would help you make new connections, communicate effectively, or assert yourself.

. . . the victim of your own unrealistic expectations—negative ones that increase your anxiety and convince you to avoid social situations or ones that leave you feeling disappointed and resentful.

. . . so preoccupied with your own moods and problems that you do not stop to consider the effect you have on other people and unintentionally drive them away.

. . . looking for acceptance, approval, and comfort from people who are incapable of providing it at all or only under specific circumstances, and overlooking or not taking full advantage of the sources of emotional support that are available to you.

Clinical researchers have observed these forces at work in the lives and relationships of people with mood disorders, including DD. Depressed individuals inadvertently sabotage themselves at every turn and frequently avoid social opportunities, withdrawing from friends and family, and leading lonely, isolated existences—all of which adds to and sustains their depressed mood. Conversely, when sufferers are helped in the effort to conquer social anxieties, modify their expectations, explore their options, and identify new sources of support, the dynamics of depression can be, to a large degree, turned around. The following will help you pinpoint some of your interpersonal "glitches" and begin to correct them so that you can start to benefit from the mood-elevating pluses other people and your relationships with them have to offer you.

GLITCH #1: BASIC SOCIAL SKILLS

As you may recall, Joel spent a good deal of his time reminiscing about the "good old days" and wishing that he and his life could once again be the way they were during high school and college. Back then, Joel always had a group of friends around him, and those friends brought new people into his social circle and planned social activities. All Joel had to do was show up and enjoy the benefits. Taking it for granted that there would "always be something to do and someone to do it with," Joel developed a pattern of social passivity that caused no problems while his friends were doing all of his social groundwork for him. But when Joel graduated from college and moved to San Francisco, he lost that social safety net. Being alone in a strange city and missing the people with whom he had effortlessly felt secure and accepted was, as Joel put it, "quite a shock to the system." It was a shock Joel assumed would "just wear off" one day. "I figured that once I settled in and got my bearings, things would pick up," Joel said. "I kept telling myself, 'Just wait it out. Give it some time. Good stuff will start happening eventually.' "

Halfway through his sixth year of "waiting it out," Joel realized that the conditions from his college days were not going to magically re-create themselves and that his social needs would not be fulfilled unless he took action to meet and get to know new people. Much to his dismay, Joel also realized that he had never learned how to do that. As he put it, "When it comes to socializing, especially with women I'd like to date, the average sixteen-year-old has an edge on me."

Of course, Joel's situation was not as hopeless as he thought it was. Like foreign languages, gourmet cooking, or playing the piano, the basic techniques for getting to know and getting along with other people are not talents you are born with but are skills you learn and polish through repetition. You might not have learned them previously, or they may have gotten rusty during the years that you have been down in the dumps. But if you are willing to give them a try or practice, practice, practice, you can build a repertoire of skills that will serve you in almost any social situation. Take out your notebook and try the following.

TAKE A SOCIAL SKILLS INVENTORY. List the skills you would like to develop or improve. Identify your top five by assigning the number 1 to the skill you would like to work on first, the number 2 to the skill you would like to work on next, and so on. When it comes to dealing with other people personally or professionally, casually or intimately, on a one-time or an ongoing basis, what do you wish you could do that you have not been able to do at all or as well as you would like to? Some of the skill deficits prevalent among DD sufferers include conversing with someone you just met, accepting compliments, flirting, initiating conversations, expressing opinions, asking someone for a date, fending off unwanted attention, setting limits on other people's inappropriate or even abusive behavior, picking up signals that someone is interested in getting to know you, handling appropriate criticism, asking for assistance, being specific, choosing social activities and inviting people to join in them, saying no, listening to other people talk about their feelings, negotiating compromises, dealing with differences of opinion or conflict.

EMPLOY THE FOLLOWING SKILL FOR ALL SEASONS— LISTENING. A universal demon that haunts people who lack confidence in their social skills is the one captured in the claim "I never know what to say," and the question "But what if I can't keep up my end of the conversation?" Countless self-help books offer advice on how to exorcise that demon, telling you how to do everything from coming up with great opening lines to carrying on intimate conversations. Some of those resources are found in the appendix under Behavior Therapy. You may also want to give *active listening* a try. It is effective (and anxiety-reducing) in almost any social situation or personal interaction.

You are listening actively when you focus on the other person's words and actions instead of worrying about what to say next (or what you are going to eat for lunch or how far behind on your housework you are). By concentrating on what is being said and what is being conveyed to you nonverbally through facial expressions, tone of voice, and body language, you will always have something to say because the second part of active listening is responding in a sympathetic nonjudgmental way. Rephrase or restate the other person's message as you understood it without ridiculing, criticizing, or immediately turning the spotlight on yourself. "It sounds like you're a real Cubs fan," "Your job sounds very challenging," or "I know what you mean. It is tough unwinding after such a hectic day" are examples of reflective responses to another person's statements.

Reflecting and paraphrasing in this way is particularly effective in emotionally charged situations like the one Beverly encountered when her daughters announced that she "had to" drive them to the mall. Instead of losing her temper and going on a tirade, she might have said, "What I hear you saying is that you made plans to go to the mall and now you need a way to get there. It sounds as though you expect me to drop everything and drive you there." Then she could have given her daughters an opportunity to verify her perception or clear up any misunderstanding by asking, "Is that what you meant?" Whether Beverly's daughters acknowledged their unreasonable expectation, clarified it by saying that they would *like* her to give them a ride, or admitted that they had not considered her circumstances at all, the door for clearheaded conversation and the discussion of various alternatives would have opened and a constructive resolution of the conflict would have been possible. The interaction may not have had a perfect ending, but it certainly would have turned out better than it did when Beverly became agitated, ran after her daughters, disrupted her entire day, and felt miserable because of it.

Although it is in your best interest to continue to listen throughout most conversations, at some point you will want to move beyond reflective responses. Glib repartee is not required. Try asking additional questions, discussing how you feel about what you heard, sharing a similar experience you have had, or suggesting alternative points of view.

GLITCH #2: PASSIVITY AND THE INDIRECT APPROACHES

Because of powerful needs to please, obtain other people's approval, and avoid conflict, you may play a passive role in your relationships, rarely making decisions, voicing your opinions, negotiating on your own behalf, or protesting when more aggressive individuals steamroll right over you. As Danielle did when Greg made travel plans without consulting her, you swallow your true feelings and remain silent. For what appears to be the worthy cause of "not making waves" or "hanging on to what you have," the result is that you feel more powerless and victimized than ever.

Or because you already feel powerless and incapable of obtaining what you want or need from other people, you may use indirect, manipulative, or passive-aggressive tactics to get your own way. You may pout, sulk, or send mixed messages: "It's okay. You go ahead and have a good time. I'll be fine here all by myself" is said with a quivering lower lip, in a depressed tone of voice, and with a heartfelt sigh conveying the exact opposite. You may "mess up" or "forget" tasks that you did not want to do in the first place or ask so many questions about how to do them that the other person becomes frustrated and does the job himself.

Playing on other people's awareness of your depressed condition, you may stop them in their tracks with statements that are loaded with frightening or guilt-inducing implications: "You're the only person I can depend on. If I lost you, I don't know what I might do." Then there's the great disabler: opening lines such as "If I tell you, you'll just get angry at me" and "You won't understand." The other person promises not to do what you have predicted he will, and you are home free. Either he has to swallow his true feelings when you reveal something that warrants a negative reaction or he has to express those feelings, at which point you say, "See, I told you that you would . . ." making him the "bad guy" and taking the pressure off you.

You may "fall apart": going along with whatever someone else wants and then collapsing at a crucial moment. For instance, after Dan was awarded his free trip to the Bahamas, Connie—who "was not up for" a vacation—raced around taking care of all the necessary details in preparation for their trip. Then, not five minutes after they had checked into their hotel, she got a migraine headache from which she never quite recovered during their entire stay. Stoically, while lying in bed with the curtains drawn, she encouraged Dan to enjoy himself, but of course he couldn't.

Or you may act in ways that provoke other people's anger and then play the innocent victim of their seemingly irrational rage or resentment—as Marcia did when she forgot that she turned off the bell on her telephone and was "absolutely shocked" by Jack's reaction when he finally reached her.

Some indirect tactics—including Connie's "fall apart" and Marcia's telephone maneuver—are not consciously planned or knowingly aimed at making other people miserable. Indeed, many seemingly willful manipulative ploys are automatic—habitual behavior patterns motivated by needs and wishes that are buried in your subconscious. Consequently, you truly do not understand why people get upset with you. You engage in other maneuvers—making guilt-inducing statements or giving some-one the silent treatment—with full knowledge of what you are doing and why, but either way your ploys are rarely effective in getting what you want or need over the long haul. You often feel ashamed of your behavior, putting yet another dent in your beleaguered self-esteem. And when that behavior backfires, you are left in the same powerless, victimized position as the person who does nothing on his or her own behalf.

FIND YOUR BOTTOM LINE. If you have remained passive in your relationships or relied on indirect tactics during most of your in-teractions, before you can use more effective strategies to get what you need or want you must develop a clear idea of what those wants, needs, wishes, and desires are. In your notebook create columns or pages for the significant people in your life and then ask yourself what you want or do not want from them. What treatment is and is not acceptable to you? What do you wish there was more or less of? For each individual jot down the answers to these questions. Try to be as reasonable and realistic as possible. Your bottom line is not a grandiose fantasy about a perfect relationship but, rather, an indication of what you do not want to live with or without. Being consulted about plans that involve you, being asked rather than told you have to, having problems discussed behind closed doors and not in front of your co-workers, sharing mutually agreed upon household chores, not being physically, verbally, or emotionally abused—these are all examples of bottom-line needs, wants, and wishes.

Naturally, simply knowing what they are does not mean you will be able to fulfill them or that you should—other people have bottom lines of their own. Sometimes you will put aside your desires in favor of some-one else's. Sometimes you will remain steadfast. And sometimes you will negotiate compromises that allow both of you to get some of what you want. The next time you approach someone or are in the midst of a discussion that seems to be going awry, try to identify what you want, what you do not want, and which items are worth perseverance.

Once you know your bottom line, you can weigh your wants and wishes against the motives that got you into trouble in the first place: the need to please, the desire to avoid conflict and wanting other people's approval. There is nothing wrong with needing or wanting these things—everyone does to a certain extent—but your interactions have perpetuated your chronic case of the blues because you have allowed those needs to override all others. Now you have a conscious choice to make, and it is not an easy one. Will you adhere to your bottom line and risk disagreeing with, displeasing, or garnering the disapproval of other people? Or will you compromise your bottom line, avoiding those negative consequences but also settling for the crumbs that other people may or may not toss in your direction? You will not make the same choice in every situation, but your chances of making a choice that is in your best interest have improved now that you know where you stand.

MAKE MORE DIRECT REQUESTS. Coming right out and asking for what you want does not guarantee that you will get it. However, using a direct approach will be no less (and in all probability more) effective than your indirect maneuvers and with fewer negative repercussions. And it will always be an improvement upon doing nothing.

Asking for what you want is best suited to specific, clearly defined requests. Asking your boss to give you more autonomy, your spouse to be more supportive, or your mother to give you more space will not get you very far because you put the ball in the other person's court, and too much time can pass before it is returned. When you make such vague, general requests, other people cannot possibly understand what you actually want and will be unable to comply. So be specific. After finding out when your boss wants a progress report or a task completed, ask him if he would wait until that deadline before checking up on you. Ask your spouse to be responsible for dinner twice a week or to let you get your whole story out before giving you advice or anything else that fits your description of being supportive.

Start with small requests. You are not used to making them, and the people in your life are not used to receiving them from you. Make sure your requests are reasonable. If you pass the dry cleaner on the way home from work but your spouse has to drive twenty minutes out of his way, pick some other way for him to be supportive. When your children have only five minutes to get to their destination this is not a reasonable time to request that they find a ride.

Do not make demands. A reasonable request gives the other person the option of saying no or negotiating a compromise. Sometimes it helps to explain why you are making a request, but that is not a requirement. You have a right to ask, regardless of your reasons.

Start practicing this new skill immediately. In your notebook list twenty possible requests you could make. These should be of relatively minor importance, such as asking a cashier to change a twenty-dollar bill, your spouse to change a light bulb, your neighbor to return your lawn mower, a co-worker to proofread something, a bank teller to give you your account balances. Try to make three such requests a day for the next week or so, then move on to slightly larger issues. Finally, just do it when a need arises.

PRACTICE SAYING NO. Failing to tell people that you do not want to do something contributes to your sense of powerlessness and exhaustion; it also saddles you with a schedule overloaded with obligations. You will also derive little satisfaction from the things you do want to do because the lingering effects of your unassertive behavior will leave you either rushing around to get things done or overflowing with resentment. Worst of all, you will find other ways not to do what is asked of you or to punish the person who made the request you could not refuse, creating unnecessary conflict and heartache. Needless to say, none of this will help you overcome the blues.

Although it may make you uncomfortable to do so, you do have a right to say no. Although the person you refuse may be unhappy about it, you are not responsible for keeping him or her happy at your own expense. Neither of these concepts is particularly easy for a previously unassertive person, so it is in your best interest to get plenty of practice saying no to small requests before you tackle more emotionally charged issues.

SET LIMITS ON INAPPROPRIATE BEHAVIOR. Think of the last time someone went too far—when someone made plans without consulting you, informed you that you had to do something, lied to you, yelled at you in public, kept criticizing you long after you had apologized for the mistake you made, and so on. Imagine that you are talking directly to that person and complete the following statement:

I feel _____ when you _____
       (how you felt)   (the behavior in

_____. I would prefer you to _____
    question—be specific)   (an acceptable

_____.
    option)

This is the basic formula for behavioral limit setting, and although it does not guarantee behavior change, it does increase the other person's awareness of his or her effect on you, open channels of communication, and page the way for negotiation and constructive conflict resolution. It also reduces the harmful side effects of ignoring your feelings and tolerating behavior that is insulting, hurtful, or abusive.

GLITCH #3: SOCIAL ANXIETIES AND AVOIDANCE

Several weeks after her birthday party, Judy's co-worker Wendy mentioned that Pete, the Cubs fan with whom Judy had conversed and then run from, had been asking about her. "He said that he'd like to see you again," Wendy said, followed by: "Why don't I invite you both over for dinner one night?" Judy, who could hardly believe this news, told Wendy she would let her know when she was free for dinner, but she never did. Although she readily acknowledged that she had "missed a great opportunity to be with a great guy" the last time, Judy let a second chance slip away.

Why? "Because I knew it would never work out," Judy explained. "I'd only get tongue-tied and act dumb, the way I did the last time. He would figure out that I was all sizzle and no steak, and that would be the end of it." Since Judy thought she already knew what the outcome would be, there seemed to be no point in going through the "torture" leading up to it.

Perhaps you recognized Judy's point of view as the anticipation and negative prediction type of unproductive thinking described in chapter six. If like so many DD sufferers you are plagued by it, you perceive a potential threat to your emotional well-being, become anxious, and control your anxiety by avoiding the anxiety-provoking situation or interaction. You don't go on that blind date or to the company picnic. You don't strike up a conversation with your handsome new neighbor or ask your co-worker to turn down her radio. You don't go to new places, meet new people, or put your new social skills to use. Indeed, you may not take any social risks at all. As a result you miss out on pleasurable human contact or emotional support that would alleviate your depression. You do not get a chance to test and correct your original misperceptions. You do not learn that things rarely turn out as badly as you think they will or that you *can* cope with anything that actually goes wrong.

To conquer your social anxieties and become more open to potentially mood-elevating relationships and interactions, return to pages 102–5, read about negative predictions, and redo the worst-case scenario and reality-checking exercises you find there. Then try one or all of the following corrective measures.

DO SOME CONTINGENCY PLANNING. Pick an anxiety-provoking social situation that you tend to avoid and write it at the top of a clean page in your notebook. Then break down that situation into small pieces and list them in the order they would probably occur. Leave about five lines between each step. For example, had Judy decided to have dinner with Pete at her co-worker's home, her list would look like this:

1. Decide what to wear and get dressed
2. Do my hair and makeup
3. Drive to Wendy's house
4. Walk up to the door and knock
5. Enter
6. Awkward moment when I'm first in the room with Pete
7. Small talk and cocktails before dinner
8. Carry on conversation during dinner
9. Maintain his interest after dinner
10. Decide to leave
11. Leave

Since your avoidance of a particular situation is apt to be a reaction to your negative predictions, take a few moments to make those predictions. Draw a vertical line dividing the space below each step into two sections. In the left-hand section jot down what predictions could go wrong at each stage. Try to be as realistic as possible, eliminating any worst-case scenarios you might be tempted to include.

In the right-hand section write at least one contingency plan to prevent each of the predictions or list a way it could be handled. For example, Judy's first catastrophe involved choosing the wrong outfit, with the result that she was over- or underdressed. She decided that she could avert this disaster by calling her hostess and asking for suggestions of appropriate attire. To overcome the bigger obstacle of keeping up her end of the conversation during dinner, Judy planned to use the active listening technique described earlier.

Although it will take some thought, you too will be able to come up with *something* you can do to counteract or at least reduce the impact of each of the negative consequences you envision. Your options need not be perfect. Since most of what you fear will not occur, chances are that you will never have to use your contingency plans. Still, having them— and knowing that you could do something if the worst were to happen— will reduce your anxiety measurably.

USE RELAXATION AND VISUALIZATION TO LOWER YOUR ANXIETY LEVEL. Even with your contingency plans, how anxious do you think you will be at each stage of your social situation? Using a scale of zero to ten, with zero being completely calm and relaxed and ten being sheer panic, write your numerical rating beside each step. Expect your ratings to fluctuate rather than rise with each step. Judy, for instance, gave deciding what to wear a rating of 6 and her awkward moment a 7, but making small talk over cocktails was only a 4.

The higher your rating, the more uncomfortable you will feel and the more likely you will run from a potentially mood-elevating experience. Consequently, you should learn how to lower your anxiety level. Start by familiarizing yourself with how it feels to be at level zero. Get into a relaxed state physically and emotionally. Then begin picturing yourself going through the steps of your anxiety-provoking social situation. Whenever your anxiety-level rises above a 3, use your relaxation technique to bring you back to zero and then start over. Spend fifteen minutes a day on this process, repeating it as many times as it takes to get through the entire visualization without experiencing more than level 3 anxiety.

The process of returning to zero proves to your doubtful psyche that you can control the amount of anxiety you feel without avoiding the anxiety-provoking situation entirely. Repeating the visualization desensitizes you to the elements of the situation that typically stir up your anxiety. With each repetition it becomes more difficult to raise your anxiety level and easier to lower it. As soon as you notice this happening, it is time to go out and actually face the situation you have been avoiding. As was the case with becoming more productive, each successful visualization and actual experience builds your self-confidence and motivates you to move forward. Sooner than you think you will be taking social risks and reaping their rewards.

GLITCH #4: UNREALISTIC EXPECTATIONS AND DISAPPOINTMENT

Referring to himself as the original Clark Kent, Joel long ago gave up hope of "slipping into a phone booth and emerging as Superman." He believed that being a "mild-mannered schoolteacher" was not enough to offer a woman and that "the Lois Lanes of the world would always fall for someone else." Consequently, as he drove to his dinner meeting with Linda, the campaign manager he had met while a volunteer worker for a local politician, Joel harbored his fair share of negative expectations. Once the evening went well, however, he found the courage to ask Linda for a date (and she accepted), Joel immediately moved to the opposite extreme. After just three dates he was on cloud nine—and light years ahead of himself.

Ecstatic as well as relieved that his anxiety-provoking search for acceptance and companionship appeared to be over, Joel quickly convinced himself that Linda was "the one," the woman who would be his wife, raise his kids, live with him in suburbia, and give his life some semblance of normalcy. In his eagerness to make his fantasy a reality, he pursued Linda vigorously, calling often, showering her with gifts, rearranging his schedule so that he could spend more time at campaign headquarters, and asking her out for weeknight as well as weekend dates.

Although Linda enjoyed Joel's attentiveness at first, the intensity of his pursuit and his escalating demands on her time made Linda uncomfortable, and she tried to slow things down, to pull back and get some breathing room. Unfortunately, Joel missed these cues and continued to follow his fantasy script, doubling his efforts to get closer to Linda each time she tried to create some distance. Linda finally called a halt to the entire process, giving Joel what he referred to as the "let's just be friends speech," which took him completely by surprise.

In a flash, Joel was back in his old, familiar position—feeling hopeless, unlovable, and of course depressed. He had been victimized by the flip side of negative predictions: unrealistic expectations.

Ironically, DD sufferers, who are notorious for their pessimism and dismal prophecies for the future, frequently raise the emotional ante on interactions by expecting more from encounters, relationships, and other people than can reasonably be delivered. When their expectations go unmet, they feel disappointed, sad, resentful, or bewildered, and their unproductive thought processes and original depressed state return. This time, however, they seem to have good cause for feeling blue: They have lost something important to them, possibly their future happiness.

One of the most common of these unrealistic expectations is the one Joel harbored—believing that someone or something will supply the happiness, self-confidence, and normalcy that cannot be found on your own. Based on little or no concrete evidence, the DD sufferer concludes that "this is it, this is what I've needed all along." Naturally, once such a miraculous cure has been found, there is great reluctance to part with it or to recognize that it might not be all that was desired.

Other unrealistic expectations that may be undermining your relationships and interactions include the following:

You expect other people to understand you and unconditionally support you. This is the basic assumption behind "If you really cared about me, you would . . ." type of unproductive thinking. It dramatically increases the emotional significance of many interactions because you are prone to see any infraction of your unwritten "rules for caring" as an omen of the impending demise of your entire relationship.

You expect other people to know what you are thinking or feeling without being told and to do what you need or want them to do without being asked. This not only puts an unfair burden on the people in your life, but since mind reading is an ability most human beings do not possess, it invariably leads to one disappointment after another.

You wish and hope for extreme closeness and unlimited reassurance. If you have been alone and lonely for any length of time and have now made a human connection, you may press for more and more of the warmth and closeness you have been lacking. Unfortunately, as Joel did, you may push so hard and cling so tightly that you drive people away. Or like Marcia, you may feel frightened and vulnerable without it and therefore seek constant reassurance that people care about and are there for you. Again, few people can provide all that you seek; they will pull back in order to protect themselves. Regrettably, their retreats trigger an automatic "try harder" reaction from you, setting off a self-defeating cycle until something has to "give"—and whatever that is, it won't be to your benefit.

You expect your relationships to be conflict-free. Somewhere along the line you came to believe that your friends, mates, children, and all those who truly care about you are supposed to agree with you at all times and never get angry or hurt, or criticize you. Assuming that the people in your life will always be on your side and that your relationships will always proceed smoothly is unrealistic.

Unrealistic expectations are always no-win propositions. If you pick up the cues that indicate how someone or something really is, then you are disappointed because reality has failed to live up to your idealistic fantasies. If you overlook or ignore those cues, you cannot adjust your behavior in ways that would make your relationships or interactions work for you. What is more, while you are trying harder and harder to fulfill your lofty expectations, you miss out on the mood-elevating benefits offered in the real world.

GRIEVE FOR YOUR LOSSES. Even though your relationship may not end or change from a romance to a friendship the way Joel's did, whenever your expectations go unmet you suffer a loss. A hope has been dashed, an illusion shattered, a possible door to future happiness slammed shut. That hurts. You feel angry, frustrated, resentful, sad, and disappointed. Allow yourself to feel those emotions. Even if it seems silly to get all worked up about something you never actually had, you do not have to reason yourself out of your feelings or keep a stiff upper lip. You can talk about them. You can even wallow, storm, and wail for a while.

What you do not want to do is generalize your emotional response to a specific circumstance so that your reaction colors your feelings about who you are as a person or your prospects for the future. Yes, you lost this round, but there are many more rounds to go and many more opportunities for success if you learn from your mistakes rather than giving up because of them. Do not make life decisions based on your temporary, albeit distressing, emotional state. When you are upset over unmet expectations is not the time to quit your job, file for divorce, decide never to attend another party, or make any other long-range plans. Wait three days. You will see things more clearly once the dust has settled.

GET IN TOUCH WITH REALITY. Before you draw any conclusions or make decisions that will have an impact on your future interactions as well as your blue mood, try to determine what is behind your pain and disappointment—the actual circumstances or the gap between your expectations and reality. Ask yourself what really happened. As you did during the self-monitoring exercise in chapter four, describe objectively the interaction as if you were watching a movie, recounting events, words, and actions as if they were happening to someone else. Then compare that version to what you wished, hoped, or expected to happen.

In some instances you will locate the root of your problem immediately. Danielle did: She quickly realized that Greg's announcement about being chosen to present a paper at an important medical conference was actually a neutral transaction. There would have been absolutely nothing disappointing or depressing about it if she had not expected to live out her fantasy of springing *her* news on Greg as soon as he sat down and then basking in his approval.

Of course, disheartening interactions are not always so clear-cut. For instance, Jack really did snap at Marcia, and his angry words had the potential to upset almost anyone. Linda really did call a halt to the romantic aspect of her relationship with Joel, and in his place almost anyone would feel hurt and rejected. Yet those facts did not automatically absolve Marcia or Joel of all responsibility or justify their perception of themselves as innocent victims. Their unrealistic expectations still played a major role in the upsetting interaction.

Even if you see yourself as the injured party, you must ask yourself how you may have set yourself up for that role. The question is not designed to induce guilt or absolve the other person. It is intended to help you identify the things you can change in order not to find yourself in the same straits in the future.

MODIFY YOUR EXPECTATIONS. Once you have identified the gap between what really happened and what you wanted to happen, take a close look at your expectations. Were they reasonable? Could you have lived up to them if the situation had been reversed? Did you make them clear to the other person involved in the interaction? Did you use a direct approach to meet them, asking for what you needed or wanted and giving the other person an opportunity to choose whether or not to comply? Did you pay attention to any early signs that the other person might not be following the same fantasy script you were? Negative responses to any of these questions are an indication that your unrealistic expectations are interfering with your interpersonal relationships. Review the cognitive strategies in chapter six and use them to refute, revise, and replace your unreasonable expectations.

While reviewing his ill-fated relationship with Linda, Joel discovered that although he liked Linda well enough for herself, he had decided she was "the one" because he desperately wanted someone to fill that role. His desire to be part of a couple, his need to relieve his loneliness, his longing to slip into a ready-made social life were such powerful incentives that, when he looked at Linda, he saw only what he wanted to see. Once Joel observed the real person and the real circumstances objectively, he realized that Linda was right. They made better friends than lovers.

In order to prevent unnecessary pain and disappointment, you need to look at the external circumstances as well. Some wishes and desires that are realistic on paper become unreasonable under certain conditions. You can be the victim of bad timing, such as calling a friend to relieve your loneliness just as he is walking out the door or right after she has learned she will be audited by the IRS. You can approach people only to discover that they are under too much stress or too preoccupied with other concerns to respond as they usually do. Or you may have neglected to consider another person's unique strengths and limitations. For instance, you might reasonably expect a boss to allow you to do the tasks she assigns without constantly looking over your shoulder. But *your* boss may be highly controlling and look over everyone's shoulder—making your expectation unattainable. If you do not want to be disappointed, you must be willing to modify even your realistic expectations whenever they do not fit a specific situation or individual.

GLITCH #5: OVERREACTIONS

Turn to a clean page in your notebook and complete the following sentences in reference to the troublesome relationships and interactions in your life.

> I hate it when . . .
> I tend to go off the deep end when . . .
> If someone wants to get on my nerves, all he has to do is . . .
> My guard goes up when . . .
> I have been known to burst into tears over . . .
> If you want to start a fight with me, just . . .
> To push my "guilt button" just . . .
> I seem to be particularly sensitive to . . .

You have just identified your sore spots. When other people's words or actions inadvertently strike or are intentionally aimed at these vulnerable areas, they prompt a knee-jerk reaction that is almost always out of proportion to the realities of the immediate situation. Sometimes your overreactions are so extreme that they make little or no sense to anyone who sees them, including you. For instance, Marcia admitted that Jack was a loving, attentive husband and that she had no "logical" reason for being so terrified of losing him.

Your areas of heightened sensitivity often represent thoughts and feelings attached to unsettling *past* experiences that are being transferred to people and interactions in the present. Although you are rarely consciously aware of the connection, you *reexperience* problems and emotions left over from previous relationships, and the combined effect of your unfinished business and your current circumstances accounts for the intensity of your reaction. That was certainly what happened to Marcia, whose fear of being abandoned by Jack stemmed from her actual abandonment by her father, who "ran off with our seventeen-year-old babysitter and was never heard from again."

You have also seen this intricate interplay of past history and present-day reality operating in both Joel's and Danielle's lives. The possibility of getting the brush-off from women he did not even know was so catastrophic for Joel because each time he approached someone in a singles bar he reexperienced the dread he felt when he tried and failed to capture his depressed mother's attention. Danielle's relationship with

Greg was virtually identical to the one she had with her perfectionist, impossible-to-impress mother. Danielle constantly tried to obtain from Greg the acceptance and approval she had not gotten during childhood.

Psychotherapy provides the most effective avenue for uncovering and completing unfinished business. However, you can help yourself by becoming more aware of your sensitive areas and more conscious of your own responses when interpersonal relations enter especially sensitive areas. Train yourself to stop and ask: Are my thoughts and feelings and what I am about to do appropriate and relevant to what is happening right now? If they are not, employ the applicable cognitive strategies in chapter six or use one of the effective social skills presented earlier in this chapter.

GLITCH #6: LOOKING ELSEWHERE FOR SUPPORT

If you make a sincere effort to employ the skills and strategies described in this chapter and your relationships or interactions continue to have a depressing effect on you, it is time to consider the possibility that you are trying to get something you need from someone who is incapable of giving it. Danielle eventually realized that about Greg. "He's just not the type of guy who gives praise or emotional support," she explained. "That's not part of his repertoire. He doesn't understand why anyone needs it or how to give it, and I don't think that's going to change." Does that mean Danielle should end her relationship with Greg? Not necessarily. There are positive things Danielle is getting from the relationship—stimulating conversation, someone who is more than willing to take charge when she becomes indecisive, a compatible sexual partner, and the encouragement, albeit sometimes harsh, to keep trying to overcome her blues. "What I need to do," Danielle said, "is stop banging my head against the wall with Greg and look elsewhere for the approval and encouragement I've been trying to squeeze out of him." Danielle did not have to look very far: Her friends, her agent, members of the art world, and her therapist had been willing to support and encourage her all along. She had simply been too absorbed in obtaining Greg's approval to notice or take advantage of those other human resources.

Expecting one person to meet all of your needs is unrealistic and unfair, especially when there are other avenues available to you. There are all sorts of self-help and support groups, twelve-step programs for recovery from addictions or compulsive behaviors, church and community organizations that can help while offering you an opportunity to socialize. You can find people who share your interests by taking adult education courses. You can find people to exercise with at your local gym. There are professional resources, including psychological services that provide additional support as well as help you overcome your chronic case of the blues. The possibilities are limited only by your imagination and your willingness to try something new.

9

Seeking
Professional
Help

I was raised to be self-reliant," Beverly said. "In fact, I got the impression that talking about your problems to outsiders bordered on being a sin. But finally I had to admit I couldn't beat this thing all by myself. I needed a push, some guidance, some objectivity." Beverly found what she needed at her local mental health center.

"I kept telling myself I wasn't that bad off," Joel explained. "I didn't see what I had to talk to a therapist about. It wasn't as if I was on the verge of a breakdown or anything." But like Beverly, Joel eventually realized that he kept running into the same brick wall. "Even though I was doing all the self-help stuff and even though things were getting better, I was missing something somewhere." After just six weeks of treatment with a psychiatrist trained in interpersonal therapy, that brick wall was beginning to crumble, and Joel could see "the puzzle pieces falling into place." The new perspective and expert advice he received from a knowledgeable and experienced professional helped Joel capitalize on the progress he had made on his own.

"I'd gone the therapy route in the past," Danielle commented. "Several times, as a matter of fact. It had never really done much for me except get me all worked up about my mother and the way she treated me. But then I never really understood what was wrong with me before." Armed with the new information she had gathered about dysthymia, Danielle made an appointment at a clinic specializing in the treatment of mood disorders. After an extensive diagnostic evaluation, she was informed that if she truly wanted to overcome her chronic depression, she would have to discontinue her alcohol and Valium use. "I was not too pleased about that," Danielle admitted, "but I was so sick of being sick that I was willing to try anything." Although she is only just beginning to work on her mood disorder, Danielle has been living drug and alcohol free for the past six months and basking in the emotional support and acceptance she receives from her fellow members of Alcoholics Anonymous.

Although Danielle, Joel, and Beverly as well as most of the others we have discussed eventually sought, found, and benefited from professional help, they initially resisted or felt skeptical about it. You may be feeling that way now. Perhaps you are concerned about being stigmatized by seeing a therapist; you may be afraid that digging around in your psyche will make matters worse or uncover some secret and some monstrous aspect of yourself that you would prefer not to know about. Or like Danielle, you may have been dissatisfied with the professional help you received in the past or doubt that more psychological services will actually do you any good.

Yet, in spite of these common and natural apprehensions, you may also recognize that you . . .

. . . are not getting better, despite trying very hard;

. . . could use more emotional support and sound advice than you are able to obtain from friends and family members, especially if you frequently feel guilty about burdening them with your problems;

. . . would benefit from the objective observations and expertise a professional therapist can provide, especially if you get confused when you try figuring things out within the confines of your own mind;

. . . need additional coping skills or strategies for undoing your unproductive thinking;

. . . seem to move forward for a while only to slip back into your old habits or run into an obstacle you cannot overcome on your own;

. . . would like to complete unfinished business from your past experiences that is influencing your present-day interactions and relationships;

. . . are too exhausted, agitated, lethargic, indecisive, or overwhelmed by other DD symptoms to start, much less stay with, a self-help program such as the one described earlier.

These are just a few of the reasons for seeking professional help, and any one of them outweighs *all* of your excuses or rationalizations not to. Therapy can and does help people lead more satisfying lives. Several types of therapy are available as well as a number of antidepressant medications that have helped thousands of men and women overcome chronic cases of the blues in relatively short periods of time. The following information will also help you find and fully benefit from the appropriate and effective professional resources that are available to you.

THE ABCs OF PSYCHOTHERAPY
Nowadays "therapy" is a household word. There are probably few Americans over the age of twelve who do not know that psychological treatment for individuals, couples, and families exists. They also know that it is provided by psychiatrists, psychologists, social workers, and other mental health care professionals who are knowledgeable about the workings of the human mind and who have training and experience in helping people cope with and overcome emotional and interpersonal problems.

If you have never been in therapy, you will be uncertain of exactly what to expect from it and, consequently, a bit frightened and confused by the prospect of trying it. And even if you have received psychological assistance in the past, your efforts to find the kind of help you need now can be anxiety-provoking and bewildering. There are a variety of therapies available, each with its own strengths and limitations. To choose the one that is right for you, begin by considering the following basic information about psychotherapy in general.

Evaluation and diagnosis are an integral and essential part of the therapeutic process. Effective treatment begins with an extensive intake evaluation to determine whether or not you have DD and to examine all of the possible factors that may be contributing to your chronic case of the blues. Because DD is such a complex disorder and so often unrecognized or misdiagnosed, this phase of treatment is vitally important. Be wary of any therapist who begins working on your problems without it.

This evaluation should include a thorough medical history to identify any illnesses that are associated with depression. A family history should also be taken. Regardless of the methods used, you can expect to be asked about your family background and previous relationships as well as to supply detailed information about your present difficulties. Intake sessions also provide you with an opportunity to find out about your therapist and his or her approach to treatment.

Individual therapy involves an ongoing dialogue between two people: you and your therapist. You form a therapeutic relationship, joining forces to work toward a common goal—resolving the problems for which you sought professional help. Toward that end you and your therapist make different but equally important contributions. You honestly express your innermost thoughts, feelings, and concerns while your therapist skillfully and supportively elicits pertinent information from you, helps you see and understand your problems from a new, more objective perspective, and guides you through your recovery process. Sometimes that process involves behavioral changes, changes in your attitude about yourself, or a combination of the two.

Group therapy also offers numerous advantages especially if your chronic case of the blues has impaired your interpersonal functioning, stirred up social anxieties, or left you feeling lonely and isolated. With one or more therapists present to facilitate the interactions among its members, a therapy group enhances your recovery by giving you an opportunity to view other people more realistically, receive feedback about the effect you have on other people, and adjust your behavior accordingly. You also get a chance to develop and practice new social skills as well as gain new insights into your problems by listening to other people talk about theirs.

Marital therapy is another option worth considering. As you know, your depression can take a toll on your marriage, and the conflicts in your marriage can contribute to your chronic case of the blues. If you choose to take advantage of this alternative, you and your partner will attend therapy sessions together.

Although being drug and alcohol free is not a prerequisite for overcoming a chronic case of the blues, drug and alcohol abuse will likely hamper your progress. Not only will the physical effects of various substances maintain your DD symptoms, but you may also try to keep your usage a secret, tying your therapist's hands and limiting the benefits you can receive from psychotherapy. Consequently, substance abuse treatment is highly recommended.

WHAT WORKS FOR DD SUFFERERS

Your best bet for overcoming the blues in a relatively short period of time appears to be a form of therapy that . . .

> . . . takes a psychoeducational approach, teaching you *about* your mood disorder, its components, its course, and its prognosis as well as helping you develop and practice new behaviors, thought processes, or social skills;
>
> . . . is directive, with your therapist taking an active role in the process—making observations, encouraging you to take responsibility for your predicament, and even giving you "homework" assignments to complete between therapy sessions;
>
> . . . enables you to identify your specific problem areas quickly, set goals for addressing those problems, monitor your own progress, and have a say in determining the direction therapy will take you;
>
> . . . is "here and now" focused and tailored to address *your* immediate concerns and specific DD symptoms. For one individual, treatment might be geared toward making career choices and being more productive at work. For another, time management and increasing pleasurable activities might be the primary goal. Someone else might work on reducing anxiety, rebuilding relationships, or being less of a perfectionist.

Of the therapeutic approaches widely practiced today, three most closely match these criteria and have produced positive results for dysthymic patients: Cognitive Behavioral Therapy, Behavioral Therapy, and Interpersonal Therapy.

Cognitive Behavioral Therapy. This is more commonly referred to as *Cognitive Therapy*. It was originally developed by Dr. Aaron Beck and was designed specifically for the treatment of depression. Popularized in the best-selling self-help book *Feeling Good*, by Dr. David Burns, one of Beck's associates, cognitive therapy is based on the premise that how you feel is the result of how you think. By identifying, testing, revising, and replacing faulty perceptions and various thinking errors, you alter your unrealistically negative view of yourself, the world, and your future—relieving your depression in the process. The self-help strategies found in chapter six were based on the principles and practices of cognitive therapy. You can expect a cognitive therapist to help you explore similar issues and give you similar assignments.

Behavioral Therapy. In chapter seven you encountered the second therapeutic approach that has been very successful for treating depression in general and has brought relief to many DD sufferers—*Behavioral Therapy*. Based on the premise that depressed individuals behave in ways that bring about negative consequences as well as deprive them of positive experiences, behavioral therapy shows you how to change what you do in order to change how you feel. Depending on your unique needs and concerns, you might be encouraged to become more active or add more pleasurable activities to your life; learn to assert yourself, relax, and manage your time; or engage in role playing, visualization, or systematic desensitization exercises to modify your reaction to unsettling day-to-day experiences.

Interpersonal Therapy. In chapter eight you were introduced to *Interpersonal Therapy* (IPT) techniques developed by Dr. Gerald Klerman and Dr. Myrna Weissman. The "newest" of these three types of treatment for mood disorders, IPT views depression as an illness that can contribute to interpersonal problems or be caused by them and concentrates on relationships as the gateway to understanding and overcoming the blues. The overall goals of IPT are to relieve symptoms of depression, improve self-esteem, and increase interpersonal effectiveness (helping you get what you want or need from interactions and relationships in a self-enhancing rather than self-defeating way). In the process the interpersonal therapist will help you deal with personal losses, learn new social skills, and resolve conflicts constructively if those are currently problematic issues for you.

Cognitive, behavioral, and interpersonal therapies are highly structured, action-oriented approaches that focus directly on your disorder yet go beyond it to teach you coping skills that you can use in all areas of your life. They are short-term therapies that bring about positive changes in your attitude or behavior within weeks and noticeable improvement in your overall mood in as little as three months. Many practitioners combine elements of the three for an eclectic approach that can also be quite effective. In addition, all three approaches work well as part of a comprehensive treatment package that also includes antidepressant medications.

ANTIDEPRESSANT MEDICATIONS

Today a variety of medications are used to control or relieve many kinds of mental illnesses, including depression. Widely used since the late 1950s, these medications influence the way that nerve cells communicate with one another in the brain, particularly in areas regulating emotion. Antidepressants can elevate depressed moods and reduce symptoms of depression.

A thorough diagnostic evaluation (including a physical examination) is essential before medications are prescribed. Since some medications are more effective for certain individuals than others, it may take several trials and adjustments before you are matched with the drug that is best suited for you. Most antidepressants—and there is a wide variety of them available—should be monitored after they are prescribed. A psychiatrist (who can prescribe medication) or your physician will start you on a relatively low dosage and increase the dosage until the effective level is found. Because all antidepressants have side effects, it is essential to comply with your doctor's orders regarding when to take the medication and how much of it to take. If you do experience side effects like those listed in table 4, be sure to report them to your physician.

Antidepressants can be divided into two major groups: tricyclics and

MAO (monoamine oxidase) inhibitors. Traditionally, the first antidepressant medication your doctor will try will be one of the tricyclics. Named for their three-ring chemical structure, these medications include some whose brand names you may be familiar with—Elavil, Norpramin, Sinequan, Tofranil—and more than a dozen others. Tricyclics have up to an 80 percent effectiveness rate on patients suffering from major depressions.

Your physician also may prescribe one of the MAO inhibitors (MAOIs)—Nardil or Parnate.

In another category there is Prozac—the brand name for fluoxetine, a new antidepressant compound. It became available in 1987, and as of this writing it is the most prescribed antidepressant on the market. There are several reasons for this including the fact that it has fewer side effects than tricyclics or MAOIs, and does not require such close monitoring.

Once you arrive at the correct medication and the effective dosage, you should not expect to feel good overnight or in a few days. It takes

TABLE 4   DRUGS COMMONLY USED IN THE TREATMENT OF DEPRESSION

I. ANTIDEPRESSANTS

TYPE;2	GENERIC NAME	TRADE NAME(S)
Tetracyclic	maprotiline	Ludiomil
Tricyclic	amitriptyline	Elavil
Tricyclic	amoxapine	Asendin
Tricyclic	desipramine	Norpramin, Pertofrane
Tricyclic	doxepin	Adapin, Sinequan
Tricyclic	imipramine	Tofranil
Tricyclic	nortriptyline	Aventyl, Pamelor
Tricyclic	protriptyline	Vivactil
Tricyclic	trimipramine	Surmontil
Other	trazodone	Desyrel

The most common side effects are drowsiness and sleepiness, dry mouth, dry eyes, blurred vision, constipation and difficulty urinating, increased pulse, and dizziness or lightheadedness on getting up quickly. Less common ones include skin rashes, sweating, weight gain, tremors, and altered orgasmic functioning.

II. MONOAMINE OXIDASE INHIBITORS (MAOIs)

GENERIC NAME	TRADE NAME
isocarboxazid	Marplan
phenelzine sulfate	Nardil
tranylcypromine sulfate	Parnate

If your physician prescribes MAOIs, he will give you a detailed list of foods and medications you must avoid, items as diverse and seemingly harmless as yogurt, figs, cheddar cheese, avocado, chicken livers, pills for the common cold, and many anesthetics. To take this type of medication safely, you will need to familiarize yourself with this list and pay careful attention to the makeup of the foods you eat. The combination of these foods and medicines with MAOIs can lead to serious (and possibly fatal) problems with blood pressure and body temperature.

Less serious but more common side effects include dry mouth, constipation, and dizziness.

III. FLUOXETINE

GENERIC NAME	BRAND NAME
fluoxetine	Prozac

The most common side effects are headaches, nausea, insomnia, jitteriness, and weight loss. Less common are the "caffeine syndrome" (restlessness, gritting one's teeth, tremors) and decreased interest in sex.

IV. LITHIUM

GENERIC NAME	TRADE NAME(S)
lithium carbonate	Eskalith, Eskalith CR, Lithane, Lithobid, Lithotabs
lithium citrate	Cibalith-S

Side effects are nausea, vomiting, diarrhea, stomachache, tremors in the hands, thirst, frequent urination, fatigue, a dazed feeling, and muscle weakness. These side effects occur in less than 50 percent of patients, and when they do occur, most go away after several days. Side effects that come on later and may last longer include hand tremors, thirst, and frequent urination. Other side effects that require monitoring are weight gain and hypothyroidism. Infrequent side effects can include a metallic taste in the mouth, skin rash and eruptions, thinning hair, and short-term memory loss.

two to four weeks for these medications to take effect. Moreover, improvement is gradual, and the people around you may recognize it before you do. Typically, the first thing you notice is that you sleep more comfortably and that your appetite is somewhat improved. Next you will regain some of your interest in the people and events around you. Finally, you will become aware of actually feeling better. There is no "high" associated with antidepressant medication. You will not feel a burst of unnatural happiness or optimism. You simply cease being burdened by the symptoms of depression.

Lithium has proven highly effective in the treatment of bipolar disorder (manic depression). Its main effect is to moderate mood, reducing "highs" and alleviating "lows." In general, it is not as effective an antidepressant as many other medications, but it may be extremely helpful in some cases.

Abruptly discontinuing antidepressant medications can cause withdrawal symptoms, such as restlessness and anxiety. It also increases the likelihood that depression and its symptoms will return. Although you may be tempted to abandon the drugs soon after you start to feel better, resist the impulse to do anything abrupt and try to make all decisions regarding your medication in conjunction with your physician.

HOW TO OBTAIN THE HELP YOU NEED

The first question raised by first-time therapy seekers is apt to be where to find a good therapist.

Private clinics, especially those specializing in the treatment of mood disorders, are excellent resources. Many are affiliated with university medical schools.

Friends, family members, or co-workers who have been in therapy, and especially those who have received treatment for depression, are perhaps the best referral sources. When they recommend their therapist or the clinic where they received help, their information is reliable because they have observed the therapist in action. If you have seen the positive changes in them, you have additional proof of the therapist's effectiveness.

Your family doctor may be able to refer you to a therapist. The advantage here is that he or she knows you and has some idea of your preferences and personality. Your minister, priest, or rabbi is an excellent source of information as well, particularly if you want a therapist whose religious beliefs are near your own.

If you are unable to obtain a personal recommendation, community or county mental health centers are probably the next resource to try. Check the blue Government Agency pages in your local telephone book. Community mental health centers generally have a number of therapists on staff as well as well-supervised interns who provide psychological services. Since these facilities are partially funded by tax dollars, costs tend to be low. The fee is either minimal or on a sliding scale based on the patient's ability to pay.

Finally, the professional organizations and clearinghouses included in the appendix may be able to answer your questions or help you find a therapist.

HOW TO EVALUATE A THERAPIST

The more impersonal your referral source, the more carefully you will want to check out the professional whose help you are seeking. But no matter who recommends someone to you, there are certain things you will want to know and have a right to know.

It is important to know about a therapist's education and training. A therapist will generally provide this information upon request. While educational requirements for psychiatrists, psychologists, and social workers are standard throughout the United States, every state has its own licensing and certification requirements. A therapist who is licensed or certified will rarely hesitate to say so, but if you want to double-check, you can contact the state agency that handles such matters. A good therapist will also be willing and able to explain his or her therapeutic approach to you.

All of this information as well as the cost of therapy and whether the therapist's schedule can accommodate yours can be ascertained over the telephone. Speak directly to a therapist if possible (it may not be in large clinics or mental health centers). You should be prepared to give a brief description of your problem as well.

You may want your initial meeting to be a consultation rather than a therapy session, in which case the goal is a mutual exchange of information. Even though the therapist may ask most of the questions, remember that you are the one doing the hiring. And be aware that there can be mismatches despite your efforts to find the right therapist and the therapist's efforts to do preliminary phone screening. If the therapist's specialty or approach is all wrong for your problem, the reputable therapist will tell you this and refer you elsewhere. You may also want to interview more than one therapist before making a choice, just as you would interview more than one candidate for a job.

Some people walk into a therapist's office with a clearly defined idea of what their problem is and a clear-cut idea of the things they want to change about themselves. This is fine, but don't feel you must present a neat, tidy package to your therapist. You are not expected to have pinpointed your own difficulties or to have come up with a treatment plan—that's the therapist's responsibility. Moreover, people who think they know what their problem is often discover, midway through the therapy, that they were wrong. So focus on giving an honest overview of your predicament and answering the therapist's questions, which are designed to help the therapist get to know you and determine if he or she can help you.

As the therapist is gathering information, you should be making your own evaluation. Aside from the appropriate degrees and licenses, you should look for several other qualities in your therapist. You should determine if the therapist seems empathetic, seems to understand your problem and what you are going through, gives you plenty of time to express yourself, gives you the conversational space to draw your own conclusions or is pushing you toward a preconceived notion of your problem, is honest and forthright in describing things to you, knows what he or she is talking about, and does an adequate job of answering your questions.

The most important factor of all is your overall response to the therapist as a person, whether you feel comfortable with and can imagine yourself working with him or her. If not, look elsewhere.

A therapist who is impatient with you, bullies you, condescends to you, or evades your questions can be dismissed without a second session. You will never establish the rapport you need with such a person and may complicate your recovery by developing resentments about the way you are being treated.

In most instances matters will not be so clear-cut, and you may not be able to determine your compatibility in just one visit. If you merely feel doubtful, and even if you continue to feel that way for the first few sessions, try not to cease your visits right away (unless, of course, the therapist has acted in some inappropriate way). Since therapy has its uncomfortable moments, you may just have been involved in one. If after three to six sessions you still feel uncomfortable, however, discuss that fact with your therapist. If he or she is not receptive to your comments or makes no discernible effort to accommodate your preferences, you can terminate your relationship and move on.

Remember, when you seek professional help, you aren't merely a patient, you're also the boss, the person who does the hiring and firing. If you're uncomfortable or if you aren't getting the help you want, you have the power and the right to terminate the situation at any time.

You also have the responsibility to do your part to make therapy work, which does not mean just lying back while a "mind mechanic" fixes what is wrong with you. In therapy you—not the therapist—do most of the work.

Your primary responsibility is to be honest. If you are on medication, you will have to be scrupulous about taking it and even more scrupulous about reporting any and all side effects you may experience. An even more difficult task is to be honest about your feelings. It isn't easy to admit your secret fears, inadequacies, and hurts to a stranger, but talking around your concerns will only impede your progress.

There is no fixed timetable for therapeutic techniques to have results. Overcoming your blues should not be a distant promise, however; in most cases you can expect to begin feeling better within four to six weeks. But there is a big difference between feeling better and complete recovery, which will take longer to achieve. If you notice no improvement whatsoever at the six-week mark, it does not necessarily mean that you or your therapist has failed. It may tell you that it is time to try a different treatment approach or at the very least discuss some new alternatives. But please do not discontinue therapy. Simply missing the six-week or twelve-week or even six-month "deadline" for elevating your mood is not reason enough to give up on professional help. It may take longer, but if you are comfortable with your therapist, who is using one of the three approaches described earlier or a variation of them, and you are making an honest effort to get better, you will.

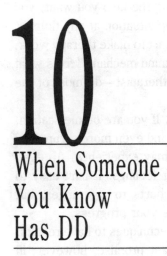

When Someone
You Know
Has DD

F or every person in America who suffers from DD there is a circle of
family members, co-workers, and friends who suffer too. If you are
part of such a circle, if you live, work, or regularly interact with someone
who has been down in the dumps day after day for years on end, you do
not have to be told how grueling an experience that can be. You already
know what it is like to feel frightened, frustrated, angered, and bewildered by a DD sufferer's behavior. You have watched helplessly as that

person's blue mood set the tone for your entire family, office, or social group. Time and again you have been taken in by a DD sufferer's tears, agitation, and vague statements about "giving up on a life that isn't worth living." And you have tried everything imaginable to "fix" things, only to end up feeling impotent and at a loss, perhaps even convinced that the chronically blue individual is willfully and maliciously manipulating you.

You cannot help being affected by someone else's chronic case of the blues, and the closer you are to the DD sufferer, the greater the impact on your life. From the outset, with whatever knowledge, skills, and resources you had, you responded to a difficult situation in the best way you could. Up to this point your best may not have been good enough to help relieve the other person's suffering or keep your own spirits up and your own life on track because the most common, natural, human reactions to chronically depressed individuals are not necessarily the most beneficial for them or for you.

POOR RESPONSES

No matter how positively motivated your efforts are, if you respond in one of the following ways, you will ride the blue mood merry-go-round *with* the DD sufferer instead of helping to slow it down.

Denial and Discounting. "When I look back now," Dan said, "I can see things that should have registered at the time, things that should have tipped me off that something wasn't quite right with Connie. Like the way she'd get all teary-eyed when she watched the evening news, especially if there was a story about something happening to a child or a family or an innocent bystander. She was fascinated with those kinds of stories in the paper too. Now I can remember her saying things like, 'No matter what you do, tragedies happen to you,' and 'No one's ever really safe.' But back then, back when Connie was starting to go downhill, I didn't hear them, or if I did, I didn't take them seriously."

On the rare occasions when Dan did notice Connie's early symptoms of DD—lethargy, fatigue, irritability, getting "all teary-eyed," or making dismal observations about herself and the world around her—he attributed them to hormonal changes brought on by Connie's second pregnancy or "naturally being a little worried about having another miscarriage." After the birth of their two sons, Dan convinced himself that the aberrations in Connie's mood were normal for someone expending a great deal of energy caring for two young children. The fact that he, his mother, and his mother-in-law were doing most of the child care seemed to escape his awareness completely. And when old friends asked what was wrong with Connie or mentioned that she seemed "sort of glum," Dan insisted that he did not know what they meant. "Everything's fine, just fine," he would say, and abruptly change the subject.

Everything was not fine, of course, but Dan could not bring himself to admit it. *Denial* was protecting Dan from *his* distressing thoughts and feelings, and it may be providing the same service for you. Or for similar reasons you may acknowledge that something is amiss but *discount* its significance, portraying the other person's chronically depressed condition as less important or meaningful than it really is.

Taking It Personally. Matthew's wife, Miriam, could vividly recall how she and Matthew used to lie in bed talking for hours; how Matthew would make her laugh with descriptions of his co-workers; how he would tell her about the projects he was working on and ask her about her day. They would trade opinions and neighborhood gossip, share their memories of childhood and their dreams for the future. Miriam missed that closeness. She missed the old Matthew. When she tried to explain why their life together held so little of the joy or intimacy that had once been so abundant, she could not help thinking that it was somehow her fault.

A sensitive and compassionate woman, Miriam felt for Matthew, intuitively understanding how drained and disheartened he was. Yet as Matthew's lethargy, pessimism, disinterest in sex, and other DD symptoms persisted, Miriam also felt guilty, inadequate, and plagued by self-doubt. What's wrong with me? she wondered. Had she let herself go? Gained too much weight? Devoted too much of her time and attention to the kids or her volunteer activities? Was Matthew withdrawing from her now because she had neglected him in the past or, worse yet, was he trying to let her know that he had grown tired of her and their marriage? As you might expect, Miriam went from blaming herself to trying to "fix" herself, doing everything she could think of to make herself a kinder, more caring and compassionate wife and irresistible partner—all to no avail. "I practically turned cartwheels to get Matthew's attention," she said, "but he still acted as if I wasn't even there."

Miriam had taken Matthew's chronic case of the blues personally, another mistake commonly made by people who are close to DD sufferers. It is difficult not to do this, because the depressed individual is withdrawing from *you,* snapping at *you,* turning down *your* social invitations or sexual overtures, and generally acting as if he or she would not mind it one bit if *you* were not involved in his or her life at all. Under those circumstances, it is tough not to feel rejected, ignored, or inadequate, but deciding that you are the problem and trying harder and harder to change yourself in hopes of making the DD sufferer happy is not the answer. It is another trap. Since the behaviors that are hurting you are symptoms of a mood disorder and not a response to anything you have done or failed to do, no amount of self-improvement will bring about the results you desire. Not only does taking things personally fail to relieve the other person's suffering, but it can do enormous damage to *your* self-esteem.

Trying to Singlehandedly "Fix" the DD Sufferer. At the same time that he was "explaining away" Connie's behavior and even after he admitted that she really was depressed, Dan "took charge" and tried to solve any problem that arose. Practical and action-oriented by nature, he switched into this "fix it" mode, attempting to make life easier for Connie by doing more and more child care and household chores, trying to cheer her up with social activities that she had once enjoyed, and giving her little hints about things she could do to feel better. He clipped articles about overcoming depression and left them on her night table. He bought her an exercise bike for her birthday. Determined to convey his love, faith, and support as well as revitalize their rapidly deteriorating sex life, Dan arranged romantic getaway weekends or got the kids out of the house so that he and Connie could have quiet candlelit dinners together. Even when these overtures were rebuffed, Dan tried to remain cheerful, optimistic, and understanding.

Dan did not mind doing any of these things. Unfortunately, they did not help, and eventually Dan's patience began to wear thin. "I saw red the day she accused me of trying to run her life," Dan recalled. "I came right out and said, 'Somebody has to. All *you* do is sit around and complain.' " He also spent the rest of the day worrying that he had "pushed Connie over the edge" and the next two weeks making it up to her by being more solicitous and helpful than ever.

If Dan's response to Connie sounds familiar to you, you may have fallen into the "fixer" trap—trying to singlehandedly "cure" someone else's chronic case of the blues only to have your well-intentioned efforts repeatedly fail or, worse yet, backfire. You may think you are being subtle, but the DD sufferer in your life generally knows what you are up to and perceives your help as criticism—more proof that he is not "good enough" the way he is. When you try to make life easier by assuming responsibility for tasks he would normally handle himself, he feels inadequate, and each time you try to cheer him up, he feels pressured. "Why can't people just leave me alone?" he grumbles to himself, withdrawing from you or pushing you away with barbed comments and angry accusations.

Although you are painfully aware that the DD sufferer is not getting better and may even be getting worse, you keep trying, intensifying your efforts each time you fail, only to fail again.

Getting Depressed Yourself. You have tried to put things right with the DD sufferer in your life; you have tried to restore the emotional climate of the relationship, but nothing has worked. After months or years of trying, you may start asking yourself whether this is what the rest of your lives will be like, whether you are ever going to be able to laugh together again, enjoy yourselves.

These queries are the natural, and some might say inevitable, outcome of watching someone you care about suffer while you are unable to alleviate the pain. They are also signs that you have begun to share the chronically depressed individual's pessimistic point of view. Having spent so much time listening to and worrying about the DD sufferer as well as trying and failing to lift the blue mood, you can start to feel as sad, helpless, and hopeless as the DD sufferer. His insidious, constant depression has gotten the upper hand and claimed another victim—you.

Because your depression is a reaction to a difficult life circumstance (being involved with someone who is perpetually down in the dumps), it is apt to come and go rather than linger indefinitely the way the DD sufferer's blue mood does. But it will be painful, and it will not do either of you a bit of good. Getting drawn into someone else's chronic case of the blues generally sends you back into one of the self-defeating cycles already described or brings you to your breaking point—when you decide not to stay but to flee.

Giving Up. Several years ago Ralph lost a "small fortune" on the stock market, leaving him in dire financial straits. Less than a month later his live-in lover abruptly ended their relationship, and he had to leave their apartment so the new lover could move in. Completely devastated by these losses, he turned to his closest friend, Sheila, whom he had known since high school. When she came to Ralph's rescue, finding him a place to live and lending him money, Sheila had no idea she was taking on a long-term project.

"I thought he'd bounce back in a few weeks, a few months at most," Sheila recalled, "but as time passed he seemed to get *more* insecure and pessimistic." Indeed, Ralph began to doubt everything about himself: his looks, his personality, his ability to practice law or hang on to his job. Sheila tried being supportive. She suggested therapy and arranged blind dates with her single friends. "But he became a totally different person," Sheila explained. "He was morose, self-centered, completely incapable of sustaining a normal relationship. And he was draining me dry."

In time, Sheila realized that she could not "save" Ralph and decided to save herself. "I sat Ralph down, made one last pitch for therapy, and then as gently as I could, I told him that he had to stop calling me, that I couldn't be there for him all the time. He seemed to take it pretty well, but I still felt horribly guilty about it. I still call him sometimes, but I keep things light. As soon as he starts to talk about how terrible his life is, I find an excuse to hang up." Sheila felt guilty about that, too, but she did not know what else to do.

Giving up on and cutting the DD sufferer out of your life is the final downspin of the spiral that began when that person first elicited your sympathy. It is the inevitable outcome of repeatedly watching your best efforts fail. And you do not always go about it as gently and sensitively as Sheila did. Indeed, in utter frustration, you may blame the DD sufferer, concluding that he is resisting your help on purpose and freely choosing to be miserable. You give up in anger with one large outburst, one loud, last-ditch attempt to shake some sense into him. And then you walk away. Or you may slip away slowly with no explanation at all: not inviting the depressed person to do things with you, not calling and making excuses to get off the phone quickly when he calls, changing the subject when he starts talking about his misery. Eventually he gets the message and virtually disappears from your life.

Although you have indeed rescued yourself from the burden your friend, relative, or co-worker has placed on your shoulders, you also lose that person and the positive things you once got from your relationship. As Sheila did, you may also weigh yourself down with guilt, feeling ashamed of yourself for "abandoning" someone at such a low point in his or her life.

As you can see, none of these instinctive responses to DD sufferers works to their benefit or yours. Neither does self-righteously judging or criticizing someone who has a chronic case of the blues. He is not being self-indulgent and weak-willed. Nor is he stubbornly refusing to "snap out of it" in order to shirk his responsibilities or get attention. Getting angry at someone whose blues won't go away does not help either. And no one wins when you decide to give a manipulative DD sufferer a taste of her own medicine by pouting, sulking, employing the "silent treatment," or trying to make her feel guilty about the people she is hurting or the tasks she is neglecting. These tactics do not solve anything but create additional problems: They make *you* miserable and perpetuate the other person's chronic case of the blues.

EFFECTIVE STRATEGIES
If you are truly interested in a DD sufferer's welfare and want to stop riding on that person's blue mood merry-go-round, you can replace your old response patterns with the following effective strategies for coping with someone whose blues won't go away.

Remember: You Are Dealing with Someone Who Is Impaired. Understanding is the key to coping with someone who has dysthymia. Because you now know a great deal about the mood disorder, its symptoms, its causes, and what can be done to overcome it, you have a clear understanding of the ailment. You must extend that understanding to the person who is suffering from that ailment, reminding yourself that even though the DD sufferer in your life looks normal, he or she has a real affliction and therefore cannot be expected to behave normally.

Recognize and Respect Your Feelings. Dysthymia changes the person who suffers from it. The chronically blue individual is not himself and does not think, respond, or behave like the person you knew and loved. The person who once joked with you, listened to you, offered you advice or a soothing touch, and was there for you in good times and bad is no longer able to do those things. The position he once occupied in your life is vacant, and you feel the impact of that loss.

Yet that person is not actually gone from your life, at least not physically. Each time you interact with the stranger who is inhabiting your loved one's body you are painfully aware that the relationship you have is *not* the one you bargained for. No amount of understanding alters the fact that you are not getting what you need from the relationship or prevents you from feeling resentful, deprived, misled, neglected, or starved for attention and affection.

What is more, when you are dealing with a DD sufferer, you are dealing with someone who can be manipulative, self-centered, hypersensitive, irritable, uncommunicative, withdrawn, and a veritable wellspring of gloom and doom. These symptoms of the mood disorder are also realities that have an adverse effect on you, stirring up feelings of frustration, anger, sadness, helplessness, or despair.

Give yourself permission to feel the way you feel. Seek out a supportive person—an objective friend, a sympathetic relative, a professional therapist—and talk about your feelings. Use the information in chapter six to gain a better understanding of how your thinking may be needlessly intensifying your feelings. And if you can do so without blaming the DD sufferer for causing them, discuss your feelings with him or her too. You will not push that person "over the edge," and you may open previously neglected channels of communication.

Learn to Detach. Detachment is the antidote for taking things personally. It is a way to stop having your buttons pushed by the DD sufferer and to start looking at your situation more objectively. Detachment is an attitude that you develop by separating the ailment from the person who suffers from it.

When someone has a physical problem such as cancer or heart disease, you are apt to feel sad about the toll it takes on that person. You get angry about the way his or her medical condition has disrupted your life. You feel helpless to relieve the suffering that the disease is causing. But you do not blame the ailing individual for your feelings or direct your anger at him. You do not conclude that he is acting sick in order to hurt you or make your life miserable. Although you get upset about the illness, you are able to remain patient, understanding, and supportive of the person who has it because you know that the person is not the same. For the DD sufferer's sake and your own mental health, you must do your best to cultivate a similar attitude about dysthymia.

Although DD symptoms often look like laziness, stubbornness, manipulation, or a willful refusal to get better, if you can manage not to confuse the two, you will be more tolerant and less resentful about blue behavior that won't go away. Although the DD sufferer's words and actions will not stop hurting you altogether, they will sting less when you remember that a mood disorder, rather than maliciousness, is behind them. When you find yourself thinking, "Why is she doing this to me?" or "If he doesn't cut that out, I'm going to throttle him," stop, take a deep breath, and remind yourself that the blues are dictating that person's thoughts and actions. Try revising *your* thoughts. Exchange "I hate him when he's like this" for "I hate this disorder for making him this way." Or "She is ruining all of our lives" for "Her depression is getting to all of us."

You also cultivate a supportive yet detached attitude by understanding what someone is going through *without* joining in and by feeling for the chronically depressed individual *without* adopting his or her point of view.

In an effort to understand and help someone who is experiencing a powerful and all-pervasive disorder like DD, you may try to put yourself in his shoes and look at the world through his eyes. Unfortunately, you can be *too* successful and not only sympathize with what that person is going through but *identify* with him and actually go through the experience too. You can align yourself with the depressed individual so completely that you accept his premises about life as valid and end up feeling as hopeless and downhearted as he does. Clearly, adopting his negative outlook as your own is detrimental to you and your emotional well-being. And because it validates the DD sufferer's unproductive thinking and blue mood mind-set, it is also detrimental to the person you are trying to help.

You do not want to go to the opposite extreme, of course, dismissing the depressed person's feelings entirely or discounting their importance. Instead, find a detached middle ground. Acknowledge and sympathize with the other person's feelings but keep them separate from your own.

Respond to what you hear but, whenever possible, skew your response to convey a slightly more optimistic perspective. For instance, you might say something like, "Yes, I can see that you feel hopeless *right now,*" which recognizes the other person's hopelessness but suggests that the feeling is temporary and could change for the better in the future. Then you might reinforce that message (and avoid joining in) by expressing your point of view: "Sometimes this situation seems huge and unmanageable to me, too, but I care for you very much and know that we can get through this together."

Accentuating the positive prevents you from absorbing the depressed individual's negativity and helps that person gain much-needed perspective. But that does not mean you should constantly play "little merry sunshine" or find fifty ways to tell someone to look on the bright side. Rather than being saccharine sweet or condescending, you can encourage the DD sufferer by pointing out progress whenever you see it and reminding him of the very same thing you are trying to remember: that DD is an illness that can be overcome.

Finally, cultivating a detached attitude enables you to accept that another person's thoughts and actions are not your responsibility. You did not give your loved one DD, and you cannot, through the force of your own will, make his or her blues go away. There are a number of specific steps you *can* take to be supportive and helpful, but those measures will not cure someone else's blues. The DD sufferer's recovery simply is not in your hands.

Try, Try Again. As far as you are concerned, everything you have ever done to help a DD sufferer should have worked. Since you would have felt better if the situation were reversed, your approach made sense to you, and you expected it to bring positive results, but it did not. And if you are like most people who are involved with DD sufferers, your immediate inclination was not to question or revamp your approach but, rather, to try again, a little harder.

There was nothing inherently wrong with that decision. In fact, because depressed individuals rarely respond to help immediately, it is actually necessary to try things two, three, or even a half-dozen times. If you try a particular strategy repeatedly, however, and see no results or, worse yet, notice the person getting more depressed, it is time to change course. If you do not, if instead you keep escalating your efforts, you will only make yourself miserable.

If what you are doing is not working, for your own sake and what is left of your relationship and the other person's sense of self-worth, try something else or do nothing for a while. When the depressed individual seems to be in a more responsive frame of mind, you can try the same approach again or attempt to get through to him in a new way.

Set Limits. By trying to comply with a DD sufferer's every wish, you will burn yourself out as well as unwittingly reward the helpless or manipulative behavior that is sustaining the other person's blues. As the behavior you are unintentionally reinforcing continues, your frustration and resentment escalate. Before you do something you will regret or feel ashamed of, try setting limits. Define your bottom line—what you can and cannot accept from your relationship or during specific interactions. Then when your bottom line is crossed, say so. Speak up on your own behalf without shouting, pounding on your desk, or attacking the other person's character.

For example, if the depressed person is calling you at work several times a day, instead of becoming outraged explain as calmly as possible why this behavior isn't acceptable. After you state your reasons, negotiate a set of new rules. Clearly, it's not acceptable to interrupt too many times every day when you are trying to work, but what will your schedule permit? One call? Two? Come up with a compromise that both of you can live with.

Setting a limit may be the easy part. Not backing down or reversing yourself is more difficult, especially since the other person probably will not automatically comply with your suggestion or request. You can expect some sort of protest in perhaps a skillful attempt to press your "guilt" button. Remind yourself that you are not responsible for another person's happiness, especially if it means sacrificing your own. Remember that by doing what you are willing to do (instead of being bullied into doing something you are unwilling to do), you ward off resentments that can poison your relationship. Although you may be afraid that the DD sufferer will have great difficulties or find a way to make you more miserable, by using effective social skills such as those in chapter eight you can strengthen your relationship and provide the other person with the means to climb out of the depths of depression.

PERTINENT QUESTIONS AND ANSWERS

Now let us respond to some of the questions that friends and relatives of DD sufferers are most likely to ask.

"The chronically depressed person in my life seems so indifferent and uninterested in doing anything. Should I insist that she join me in certain activities?"

Insisting may be too forceful an approach, and bullying, threatening, or becoming angry and accusatory definitely will not work. But you might try saying something like, "I know you may not think this will be much fun, but let's try it anyway. I'll make the arrangements and then when the time comes, you can decide whether or not you want to do this with me."

Unless the depressed person positively refuses to participate, go ahead and make plans for the two of you. Try to choose an activity that the other person used to enjoy. She may not be thrilled during the first outing—indeed, she may be silent or sullen and may later say the activity did nothing to cheer her—but as long as the person's blues do not worsen because of it, try this strategy again. She may become more interested the next time around, talking a little more and becoming a little more responsive to the people around her.

Once you're home, of course, the blue mood may return. But don't despair. If you can get a depressed person interested in something for even a brief period of time, you have made progress and have made the DD sufferer aware that it just might be possible for her to feel pleasure again.

D oes it really help to let someone talk about his blues? Couldn't dwelling on his problems make matters worse?"

The answer to both questions is yes, which is why active listening (see page 136) is an important skill for you to learn as well as for the DD sufferer. When you actively listen, you allow the DD sufferer to get his concerns and feelings out in the open, and that does help. You also gently and nonjudgmentally respond with the messages you received, and that helps even more, enabling the DD sufferer to hear himself and perhaps recognize a few unproductive thoughts. You will probably spot them right away, but please refrain from blurting out comments such as "That's stupid," "You're being irrational," "How could you possibly think that?" or "Where on earth did you get that ridiculous idea?"

On the other hand, you do not want to support the depressed person in views you think are erroneous. Listen; then, choosing your words carefully, restate. If necessary, clarify by asking the other person to explain ideas that do not fit your frame of reference. If clarifying the thought for you does not help the other person pick up the distortion, you might say, "I don't see things that way myself" and calmly explain how you do see things.

In addition, try not to offer suggestions too quickly on how to solve the problem—no matter how simple and obvious the solution seems to you. Under the influence of a chronic case of the blues, your friend or relative will automatically resist your advice and may perceive it as criticism. After you have done some active listening and have shared some of your own perceptions, you might ask the other person if he would like you to offer some alternatives. He will probably agree. If he objects to every option, do not argue your case. Let it go. At a later date, he may be more receptive to your suggestions.

I feel so helpless when the DD sufferer cries. What can I do to comfort her? Should I do anything at all?"

Crying is an expression of sadness, and since depressed people are truly sad, their tears may be an appropriate outlet. But they may be unsettling for you to witness.

The best way to comfort a crier is to sit near her and talk in a calm, soothing voice. Observations about how she must be feeling and invitations to talk about what's bothering her tend to be the most effective. Some people find physical contact soothing while others do not. You can try taking the person's hand, putting an arm around her, or stroking her hair. Make sure to ask if this touching is okay; if it is not, discontinue it.

Always offer someone who is crying the option of being alone. If that is what she wants, respect her wishes, and then return a little later to try to comfort her again or let her know where she can find you when she is ready to talk.

*H*ow can I boost the DD sufferer's self-confidence?"

No matter how highly you regard the depressed person in your life, no matter how terrific you think he is, chances are that he does not feel that way about himself. He is apt to call himself "a terrible father," "a poor husband," "an undeserving friend," or "a lazy, uninspired paper pusher who will never get ahead on the job."

You can combat this person's low self-esteem by reminding him of his accomplishments. Don't be vague here: Telling the DD sufferer that he's a "great person" isn't enough. You must be specific and validate him at random and when his self-esteem is not the topic of conversation. When he has done something good, acknowledge it when you observe it. Little comments such as, "I liked the way you explained that to Billy" or "That's a great tie; I wish I had your sense of style" can go a long way to counter the DD sufferer's insecurities and self-doubt.

You can also help a DD sufferer restore his sense of competence and capability by assisting him and offering your input as he sets goals, makes plans, organizes projects, and works through the other behavioral change strategies found in chapter seven.

I want to be there for the DD sufferer, but-maybe she'd get better faster if I wasn't. She'd have to stand on her own two feet then, wouldn't she?"

It's a mistake to think that paying attention to or agreeing to spend extra time with a depressed individual is giving in to her, babying her, or preventing her from getting better. Your presence is an excellent anti-dote to the tendency to seek withdrawal and isolation that plagues many DD sufferers. And knowing that you are nearby and available can be extremely comforting to someone whose blue moods seem to worsen when she is left alone. So feel free to give the depressed person in your life as much of your personal time as you care to. And don't worry about having to do something special during that time: It's just being there that counts.

O nce the DD sufferer is in therapy, should I just sit back and relax? Or are there things I can do to help?"

Your first reaction when you learn the depressed person in your life has decided to go into therapy may be relief that you won't have to handle this alone. But your second thought may be slightly less enthusiastic, even anxiety-filled. You may wonder what role you will be expected to play. Or, worse, whether the patient and therapist will become co-conspirators and blame you for the depression.

Relax. A reputable therapist is not interested in finding a villain to blame for someone's chronic case of the blues. If the DD sufferer is concerned about the relationship, it will probably be discussed so that the depressed person can examine its contribution to her blue moods as well as her contribution to any relationship problems that do exist. The therapist may even suggest that you and your partner go into counseling together to negotiate a new, healthier way of relating to each other. But you have the right to refuse.

Even if you are not included in the other person's therapy sessions, you may want to talk to her therapist. The therapist will not violate the patient's confidentiality. Therapy, however, may stir up thoughts and feelings that are initially difficult for the DD sufferer to handle, causing her mood to worsen. This common occurrence is temporary, but while it lasts you are apt to worry about your friend or relative and feel uncertain about how to treat that person. That is a valid reason for contacting another person's therapist. If you live, work, or regularly interact with someone who is taking antidepressant medication and are worried about the side effects you have noticed, you should also feel free to share your concerns with that person's therapist. Under those circumstances the therapist will generally be able and willing to reassure you as well as offer a few suggestions for coping with a DD sufferer who is in therapy.

Perhaps the best way to be supportive of someone in therapy for DD is to use the information obtained from this book to reinforce the attitudes and behaviors that the DD sufferer acquires during therapy session. But do not simply appoint yourself someone else's co-therapist. Check with the real therapist, asking simply and directly,

"Is there anything I can do?" The therapist will give you a clear-cut answer.

E quipped with information about dysthymia, you can now effectively cope with someone whose blues won't go away and assist that person in the recovery process. You are, however, more than a helper. You are also someone who has felt the impact of living, working, or regularly interacting with a person who has been depressed for years. You undoubtedly need and deserve to spend some time and energy taking care of yourself.

Try to resist the temptation to put your own life on hold in order to be there for the DD sufferer. Do not forgo pleasurable activities or neglect your other relationships. They are sources of satisfaction that can refresh your spirit and replenish your energy, and that may be more important now than it ever was before. If you previously turned to your depressed friend, spouse, or lover for nourishment, you will need to look elsewhere for the emotional support that is not provided at the moment. You may have to find a new exercise buddy or a different colleague to turn to for advice. You may want to join a support group. And you could probably benefit from getting some counseling for yourself.

You can also take care of yourself by learning more about your own and your loved one's problems. Psychology and self-help books like the ones listed in the appendix are excellent resources for your continuing education.

11

Personal Stories: Progress Reports

D uring the tumultuous sixties, the slogan "Not to decide is to decide" was a plea to take a stand on the social and political issues of the times. Yet it holds just as much meaning today and is applicable to anyone who has a chronic case of the blues. If you do not decide to do something about your long-lasting, low-grade depression, you are by default deciding to stay down in the dumps for another day, another week, or another year.

The knowledge and understanding you developed while reading this book makes overcoming DD possible, but your recovery process begins in earnest when *you* choose to put your knowledge to use, when you decide to take one step in any direction other than the one in which you have been traveling for far too long. The DD sufferers mentioned in this book made that choice. They did not take the same first step. They did not travel the same path at the same pace or obtain the same results in the same amount of time. Once they moved off dead center and began thinking, acting, and interacting differently than they had in the past, however, their blue moods lifted and their lives improved.

"I didn't think it was possible," Andrea wrote in a progress report.

> I didn't think my blues would ever go away. I was sure my depression and low self-esteem would be with me for the rest of my life. But I reached a point where I was so sick of my life and so sick of hearing myself complain that I was willing to try anything, so I went out and got a notebook, picked up my pencil, and started doing the self-help exercises. At first I hated all that writing, really hated every minute of it. But I forced myself to do it, and it did help. I had no idea how upside down and backwards I turned things inside my head. When I put my thoughts on paper and saw them in black and white, sometimes I practically laughed out loud at how I tied myself up in knots because of my convoluted thinking. After a while I actually started to look forward to writing, and ever since I finished therapy a few months ago, my notebook has been my therapist. When I catch myself about to go off the deep end again, I write down my thoughts, and I almost always find the "glitch"—as you call it—and can usually correct it.

According to Andrea's update, as time passed she spent less and less time consciously working on her unproductive thinking and primarily focused on changing her behavior. Cleaning out her bedroom closet motivated Andrea to take on other projects as well.

> I keep a master list of things I want to accomplish. "Little things like renewing my driver's license, long-term projects like learning to speak Italian, and fun things too. The list helps me organize my time and stick to my plans. But what I really like is checking things off when I get them done. Sometimes I go back through the notebook just so I

can look at all the check marks. They prove that I *can* cope, that I *can* get things done, and that helps me feel good about myself.

Andrea's "little" projects even led her back into the fashion business. After selling some of her clothes to a vintage clothing store, she began buying secondhand clothes at garage sales and flea markets and selling those garments as well. Then she took a part-time job at the store and eventually quit her office job to manage a second store that was opening in another part of the city. Her goal is to open her own shop specializing in clothing from the forties and fifties, and she is already making plans for that dream to become a reality. Andrea's report continued:

> I don't want to make it sound like everything I tried was a rip-roaring success. It wasn't. But looking back, the wrong turns I took taught me as much as my successes did. I didn't let them become major set-backs. I didn't give up everything over one little mistake the way I used to when I was down in the dumps all the time. I guess you could say I finally learned that I was in charge of my life and my moods, which meant that no matter what went wrong, I didn't have to take up permanent residence in the pits.

Andrea had come a long way since the days when she used her low self-esteem as an excuse not to do anything to help herself feel better. Her outlook, behavior, even the circumstances of her life had changed dramatically. Yet none of those changes occurred overnight. During the nine months Andrea spent working to overcome DD, her progress was measured in inches, not miles—and yours will be too.

Rather than waking up one morning to neon lights flashing and sirens wailing in celebration of the sudden disappearance of your blues, your mood will lift gradually. Slowly, almost imperceptibly at first, you will feel less burdened, less pessimistic about the future, less paralyzed and inadequate. You will notice that you are accomplishing a bit more during the day and sleeping a bit more peacefully at night. Depressing thoughts that once ran repeatedly through your mind are less pervasive and easier to refute, revise, or replace. Other people begin to treat you differently. They seem more cordial, more supportive, more fun to be with—all signs that you, not they, have changed. Sometimes you will feel happy, sometimes merely content, and although you will still feel blue from time to time, those moods will not last as long or seep into all areas of your life.

But remember, all of this takes time. It takes time to uproot the old habits and to practice new thought and behavior patterns until they become the norm.

"I can't say I'm my old optimistic, energetic self again," Connie reported. "But, Lord knows, I'm better than I was a year ago." According to both Connie and her husband, Dan, signs of progress became apparent more slowly than either of them expected. "It took me a long time to get rolling," Connie explained. "I'd do a few of your exercises and start feeling a little better, but then I'd get stuck. There was something getting in my way, something that kept stopping me. Dan would look at me sadly and say, 'You were doing so well. What happened?' And I couldn't answer him. I honestly didn't know the answer. Finally, I realized I'd never know unless I got some outside help."

Connie spent six months in individual therapy and an additional six weeks in marital therapy with Dan. During that time she uncovered the fundamental issue that had been fueling her depression—the miscarriage she had years earlier and the accompanying feeling that she was powerless to protect herself from harm. Once she worked through that unfinished business, Connie recognized that we cannot protect ourselves from everything. Life is risky. Anything worth doing is risky. "I lost sight of that," Connie admitted. "I forgot that taking risks wasn't just about losing, it was about gaining and enjoying and succeeding too." From the moment Connie grasped that idea, she made rapid progress. "I still have a long way to go, but I have faith that I'll get there. After all, I've come pretty far already."

Connie's update raises two important points. First, when monitoring your own progress, it is essential to keep in mind how far you've come rather than how much further you have to go. Although having a goal or an ideal version of yourself to work toward can be helpful, that goal will often seem dreadfully far away, which can cause you to overlook the actual progress you have made. So when you want to see how you are doing, compare yourself to the way you were *before* you embarked upon your road to recovery.

Second, your effort to overcome the blues will not proceed without a hitch. Like Connie, you may come across a piece of old, unfinished business that needs to be resolved before you can forge ahead. Or you may encounter new problems.

For instance, Ralph reported that he was finally getting his confidence back and his life under control when his dad had a heart attack and the whole family went into a tailspin. "He pulled through and he's doing fine, but for a while there it was practically impossible not to dwell on depressing subjects like my own mortality or how powerless I was when it came to helping my dad or comforting my mom or doing anything except waiting around to see what happened."

To further complicate matters, soon after Ralph's father was released from the hospital, Ralph was assigned a case that "F. Lee Bailey couldn't have won." To top things off, Ralph's old girlfriend contacted him, claiming that she wished she had never ended their relationship and suggesting that they try again. They did, and according to Ralph, "It was a major mistake. The best thing I can say about it is that we figured it out pretty quickly and called the whole thing off before it got too far."

As you might expect, the crisis, stress, and disappointment Ralph encountered slowed his recovery process considerably. "I was just treading water," Ralph admitted. "But as one of my colleagues pointed out, at least I didn't go under." And to Ralph's credit, once things settled down he started working on his self-help program again.

Life does not stop and wait for you to overcome DD. Real life comes with all sorts of circumstances to test your mettle and—if you are not careful—threaten the progress you have made. Even in the best of times, life's setbacks and disappointments can be hard to take. But if you are recovering from the blues, they can be especially perilous. You are still rebuilding your fragile sense of self-worth, still replenishing your energy, so you should feel free to "coast" for a while, to "tread water." But please do not put your life or your recovery on hold for long. Get moving again as soon as possible because if you do not, you are liable to find yourself back on the blue mood merry-go-round.

Remember that you may have to try several different approaches to recovery before you find one that works for you. The first two therapists Beverly consulted had very little experience treating DD, and she did not feel comfortable with the third. Then after she finally chose a therapist, she had to revise her expectations about therapy itself: "I didn't realize there was so much to it. I was ready to talk about my problems for an hour once a week, but I was not thrilled about doing homework assignments, keeping a journal, and things like that. My therapist kept saying, 'I don't have a magic wand to wave and make your problems go away. I can't fix you. All I can do is help you help yourself.' Eventually that sunk in and therapy did help."

Since raising her two teenage daughters was a source of distress for Beverly, an effective parenting course also helped. So did a support group for single and divorced parents. "I'd have to say that helped the most," Beverly explained. "It was very reassuring to hear that other people were going through the same struggles I was. I needed to know that those struggles came with the territory and weren't all my fault. Besides, it was great to be able to get out and socialize with people who understood and accepted me. I finally felt as if I fit somewhere, and that felt good."

Danielle has remained sober and has become more assertive. She is still involved with Greg but views their relationship more realistically and tries not to look to Greg for things that he cannot provide such as emotional support and encouragement. In treatment at the clinic that specializes in mood disorders, Danielle has learned techniques for managing her anxiety and has begun to make more decisions for herself. "I'm still too dependent on other people's approval," Danielle acknowledged, "and I'm still too hard on myself whenever I make the slightest mistake. But I'll get to those things sooner or later. The important thing is that for the first time in my life I actually get through entire days without getting depressed."

Matthew began making progress after he started taking antidepressant medication. "My blues were at least partially biochemical," he explained. "Once the medication relieved most of my symptoms, I could see the bad habits I'd developed over the years and started changing them. Miriam has been a tremendous help, and we're working hard to get our marriage back on track."

Through therapy, biofeedback, and relaxation training, Judy finally reduced her anxiety and increased her self-confidence enough to ask her co-worker to arrange that dinner with Pete, the attractive man she had met at her co-worker's birthday party. "It went better than I ever dreamed," Judy said. "We went to that Cubs game. In fact, we've gone to lots of Cubs games and plenty of other places too. Pete is terrific and he thinks I'm terrific, but then I was still quite depressed when we got together, and I've been getting better ever since. Having someone like Pete in my life helped, of course, but I wouldn't be fair to myself if I gave him all the credit. This hasn't been easy, but I keep reminding myself that even on my worst days now, I'm not as bad as I used to be—and I keep plugging away."

By the time Joel completed sixteen weeks of Interpersonal Therapy, he had begun to develop a social network that continues to grow and to inject joy and excitement into his once dreary life. "I've kept up my racquetball games with one guy I work with," Joel reported. "And I co-own a sailboat with three others. They had a few good laughs teaching me how to sail, but now I'm pretty good at it and get out on the bay with them as often as I can." Joel continued his political activities and is extremely enthusiastic about the environmental action group he recently joined. And although he has not met the woman of his dreams, he is dating occasionally and getting to know women as "people first and not just potential girlfriends."

Joel added, "I still get the blues once in a while, but who doesn't? At least I don't have them for weeks or months at a time anymore. Sometimes I just go with them. You know, wallow and hold a pity party where I'm the guest of honor. But then I give myself a kick and get moving again—now that I know how."

You also know how. If you take that first step in a new direction and keep "plugging away," even when change does not come quickly or easily, you, too, will overcome your chronic case of the blues. It does not take a miracle, just a decision to put your newfound know-how to work for you plus the determination to stay with it. If Andrea, Connie, Ralph, Beverly, and the others can do it, so can you.

Appendix

To obtain additional information about dysthymia or other mood disorders and mental health problems and to find out about treatment resources available in your area, contact the following national organizations, agencies, or clearinghouses:

AMERICAN PSYCHIATRIC
  ASSOCIATION
Division of Public Affairs
1400 K Street, N.W.
Washington, DC 20005
(202) 682-6200

THE CENTER FOR COGNITIVE
  THERAPY
Room 602
133 South 36th Street
Philadelphia, PA 19104
(215) 898-4100

DEPRESSION AWARENESS, REC-
 OGNITION AND TREATMENT
 PROGRAM (D/ART)
National Institute of Mental Health
5600 Fishers Lane
Rockville, MD 20857
Attn: D/ART Public Inquiries

NATIONAL DEPRESSIVE AND
 MANIC-DEPRESSIVE
 ASSOCIATION
Suite 505
53 West Jackson Boulevard
Chicago, IL 60604

NATIONAL MENTAL HEALTH
 ASSOCIATION
1021 Prince Street
Alexandria, VA 22314–2971
(703) 684-7722

NATIONAL SELF-HELP
 CLEARINGHOUSE
33 West 42nd Street
New York, NY 10036
(212) 840-1259

The following books and audiocassette tapes are also recommended:

DEPRESSION

"Beating the Blues." Editors of American Health Magazine. A taped interview with Dr. Frederick K. Goodwin and Dr. Robert M. A. Hirschfeld of the National Institute of Mental Health. Available by sending $9.95 plus $1.90 shipping to American Health Products, Dept. 280302, P.O. Box 11249, Des Moines, IA 50340. Or call toll-free: 800-624-6283.

DePaulo, J. Raymond, and Ablow, Keith. How to Cope with Depression. New York: McGraw-Hill, 1989.

Papolos, Demitri F., and Papolos, Janice. Overcoming Depression. New York: Harper & Row, 1988.

Rosenthal, Norman E. Seasons of the Mind: Why You Get the Winter Blues and What You Can Do About It. New York: Bantam Books, 1989.

Rush, John. Beating Depression. New York: Facts on File, 1985.

COGNITIVE APPROACHES

Beck, Aaron T. Depression: Causes and Treatment. Philadelphia: University of Pennsylvania Press, 1972.

———. *Cognitive Therapy and the Emotional Disorders*. New York: International Universities Press, 1976.

Burns, David D. *Feeling Good: The New Mood Therapy*. New York: William Morrow, 1980.

———. *Nobody Is Perfect* and *Feeling Good About Yourself*. Audio tapes, numbers 20268 and 20269 of the *Psychology Today* Series.

INTERPERSONAL THERAPY

Klerman, Gerald L., Weissman, Myrna M., Rounsaville, Bruce J., and Chevron, Eve S. *Interpersonal Psychotherapy of Depression*. New York: Basic Books, 1984.

BEHAVIOR THERAPY

Lewinsohn, Peter M., Antonuccio, David O., Steinmetz, Julia L., and Teri, Linda. *The Coping with Depression Course*. Eugene, Ore.: Castalia Publishing Company, 1984.

Meichenbaum, Donald. *Cognitive-Behavior Modification: An Integrative Approach*. New York: Plenum Press, 1977.

Index

ABOUT THE AUTHOR

Robert M. A. Hirschfeld, M.D., is professor and chairman of the Department of Psychiatry and Behavioral Sciences at the University of Texas Medical Branch at Galveston.

An expert in the diagnosis, clinical course, and psychosocial aspects of clinical depression, Dr. Hirschfeld has devoted much of his career to the understanding of people's susceptibility to depression. He was the project director for the largest study on the classification and follow-up of depressed patients ever conducted.

Dr. Hirschfeld graduated from the Massachusetts Institute of Technology in 1964, received his M.D. from the University of Michigan in 1968, and completed his psychiatric residency at Stanford University in 1972. Dr. Hirschfeld's papers have been published in the *American Journal of Psychiatry*, *Archives of General Psychiatry*, *British Journal of Psychiatry*, and *Journal of the American Medical Association*. He serves on the editorial board of the *Journal of Personality Disorders* and the *Psychopharmacology Bulletin*. He has contributed to the major textbooks and review publications in psychiatry.

At the National Institute of Mental Health, Dr. Hirschfeld served as the clinical director of its Depression/Awareness, Recognition, and Treatment (D/ART) program, a national education program on the diagnosis and treatment of depression. NIMH has received over 300,000 requests for his general information pamphlet entitled *Depression: What We Know*.

He currently serves as the chief of the Scientific Advisory Board of the National Depressive and Manic Depressive Association, is a member of the board of the Anxiety Disorders Association of America, and serves on the Scientific Council of the National Alliance for Research on Schizophrenia and Depression.

Dr. Hirschfeld is married to Ellen Kingsley Hirschfeld; they have three children.